AS/A-LEVEL YEAR 1

STUDENT GUIDE

AQA

Economics

The national economy in a global context

Ray Powell and James Powell

PHILIP ALLAN FOR
HODDER
EDUCATION
AN HACHETTE UK COMPANY

Philip Allan, an imprint of Hodder Education, an Hachette UK company, Blenheim Court, George Street, Banbury, Oxfordshire OX16 5BH

Orders

Bookpoint Ltd, 130 Park Drive, Milton Park, Abingdon, Oxfordshire OX14 4SB

tel: 01235 827827

fax: 01235 400401

e-mail: education@bookpoint.co.uk

Lines are open 9.00 a.m.–5.00 p.m., Monday to Saturday, with a 24-hour message answering service. You can also order through the Hodder Education website: www.hoddereducation.co.uk

ISBN 978-1-4718-4351-8

First printed 2016

Impression number 5 4 3 2

Year 2020 2019 2018 2017 2016

This Guide has been written specifically to support students preparing for the AQA AS and A-level Economics examinations. The content has been neither approved nor endorsed by AQA and remains the sole responsibility of the author.

Typeset by Integra Software Services Pvt. Ltd., Pondicherry, India

Cover photo: gui yong nian/Fotolia

Printed in Dubai

Hachette UK's policy is to use papers that are natural, renewable and recyclable products and made from wood grown in sustainable forests. The logging and manufacturing processes are expected to conform to the environmental regulations of the country of origin.

Contents

Content Guidance

Questions & Answers

Multiple-choice questions (MCQs)

Data-response questions (DRQs)

▮ Getting the most from this book

Exam tips

Advice on key points in the text to help you learn and recall content, avoid pitfalls and polish your exam technique in order to boost your grade.

Knowledge check

Rapid-fire questions throughout the Content Guidance section to check your understanding.

Knowledge check answers

1 Turn to the back of the book for the Knowledge check answers.

Summaries

■ Each core topic is rounded off by a bullet-list summary for quick-check reference of what you need to know.

Exam-style questions

Commentary on the questions

Tips on what you need to do to gain full marks, indicated by the icon **e**

Sample student answers

Practise the questions, then look at the student answers that follow.

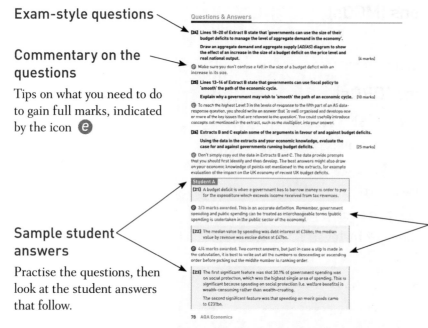

Commentary on sample student answers

Find out how many marks each answer would be awarded in the exam and then read the comments (preceded by the icon **e**) following each student answer.

■ About this book

The aim of this guide is to prepare students for the AQA AS Paper 2, 'The national economy in a global context', examination and for parts of the AQA A-level Paper 2, 'The national and international economy', examination. (The parts of the AQA A-level Paper 2 not covered in this guide are covered in *Student Guide 4*. Remember also that all the topics explained in this book could be examined in the A-level Paper 3, which is a synoptic paper testing the whole of the A-level specification.)

Content Guidance

Start off by reading the Content Guidance section of the book, which covers four separate topics. You can read all the topics, one by one, before proceeding to the Questions & Answers section of the guide. Alternatively, you may decide to read a particular topic and then the corresponding part of the Questions & Answers section. The topics follow the order of the AS Part 2 specification, starting from 'The measurement of macroeconomic performance' and finishing with 'Macroeconomic policy'.

Questions & Answers

You should read the Questions & Answers section of the book either after reading all four specification topics in the Content Guidance section, or bit by bit, having revised a selected topic on a particular part of the specification.

Multiple-choice questions (MCQs)

There are 12 multiple-choice questions (MCQs), three on each of the four topics covered by the guide. The questions are typical of those commonly set on each of the four topics covered in the Content Guidance section of the guide. Each of these questions is similar in layout, structure and style to an MCQ in AS Paper 2 and A-level Paper 3. (A-level Paper 2 does not include MCQs.) A commentary has been included after each question to explain the correct answer and any other important features of the question.

Data-response questions (DRQs)

The MCQs are followed by six data-response questions (DRQs). You can use the DRQs either as timed test questions in the lead-up to the examination or to reinforce your understanding of the specification subject matter, topic by topic, as you proceed through the Content Guidance. In this guide, the DRQs are numbered 1 to 6, but in the exams the two questions will be numbered either Context 1 or Context 2. Three of the questions in this book are in the style of AS Context questions; the other three are in the style of A-level Context questions. (Both AS Paper 2 and A-level Paper 2 require you to answer just one of the two Context DRQs in the paper.)

This section also includes:
- two student answers for each DRQ
- comments on each student's answer, explaining, where relevant, how the answer could be improved. These comments are denoted by the icon ⓔ.

This guide should be used as a supplement to other resources, such as class notes, textbooks, *Economic Review* magazine and *AS/A-level Economics My Revision Notes*. (The last two of these are published by Philip Allan for Hodder Education.) As this guide contains summaries rather than in-depth coverage of all the topics in the specification, you should not use the guide as your sole learning resource during the main part of the course. However, you may well decide to use the guide as the key resource in your revision programme. You are strongly advised to make full use of the Questions & Answers section, especially in the revision period when you should be concentrating on improving your examination skills.

Content Guidance

■ Introduction to the specification

The AQA AS specification for 'The national economy in a global context' contains the following four sections:

- 3.2.1 The measurement of macroeconomic performance
- 3.2.2 How the macroeconomy works: the circular flow of income, *AD/AS* analysis and related concepts
- 3.2.3 Economic performance
- 3.2.4 Macroeconomic policy

These also figure in the A-level specification for 'The national and international economy', though the A-level specification also includes topics covered in *Student Guide 4* and not in this guide.

3.2.1 The measurement of macroeconomic performance

The measurement of macroeconomic performance is the first in the list of topics in both the AS 'The national economy in a global context' and the A-level 'The national and international economy' specifications.

Both specifications state that students should be familiar with the various types of statistical and other data that are commonly used by economists. Data on gross domestic product (GDP), employment and inflation are often used as economic indicators. An economic indicator provides information on how well or how badly the economy is performing, in terms of achieving desired targets or goals, such as economic growth and higher living standards, full employment and control of inflation.

These and other targets, such as a satisfactory balance of payments, form the policy objectives that governments wish to achieve. It is generally best to explain how policy indicators are used to measure and assess macroeconomic performance after surveying the different policy objectives, and also the policy instruments, such as monetary and fiscal policy, that are used to try to achieve the objectives.

An economic indicator provides information on whether a particular aspect of macroeconomic policy is on course to achieve its objective. For example, data on the money supply are used to indicate the tightness or looseness of monetary policy. Too fast a rate of growth of the money supply might indicate that the main monetary policy instrument (the rate of interest) should be raised to enable the monetary policy objective (control of inflation) to be achieved.

Economic indicators are also used to compare the macroeconomic performance of the UK economy (or indeed any economy) with that of other countries. Occasionally, a data-response question in the examination may include data for four or five countries on performance indicators such as comparative economic growth rates, employment and unemployment statistics, inflation rates and trade balances.

3.2.2 How the macroeconomy works: the circular flow of income, *AD/AS* analysis and related concepts

This is the theoretical core of the specification, focusing on two interrelated macroeconomic models of the economy: the aggregate demand/aggregate supply (*AD/AS*) model and the circular flow model.

Aggregate demand in the economy is defined as the total planned spending on real national output of all the economic agents in the economy. In much the same way, aggregate supply represents the total output of real goods and services that all the firms and other producers in the economy plan to supply or sell.

AD curves and *AS* curves are brought together in the aggregate demand/aggregate supply (*AD/AS*) model of the macroeconomy. Macroeconomic equilibrium occurs at the level of real national income or output at which total planned spending equals the quantity of goods and services that firms are willing and able to supply, i.e. at the level of output at which $AD = AS$.

The circular flow model of the macroeconomy, which maps the flows of income, output and spending around the economy, also shows macroeconomic equilibrium. In this model, macroeconomic equilibrium occurs when planned injections of spending into the flow of income and spending circulating round the economy exactly equal planned withdrawals or leakages of spending out of the flow.

Students often confuse two important concepts which relate to aggregate demand: the multiplier and the accelerator. The investment multiplier measures the relationship between a change in investment and the resulting change in national income or output. By contrast, the accelerator measures the opposite relationship to the investment multiplier, namely the relationship between a change in national income or output and the resulting change in the level of investment.

3.2.3 Economic performance

The performance of the national economy can be measured by the extent to which the government's macroeconomic policy objectives have already been achieved and the extent to which these objectives can continue to be achieved in future years.

Policy objectives are targets that the government wishes to 'hit' or achieve. At all times you should remember that the ultimate purpose of government policy is to improve economic welfare, which you can think of as human happiness. More narrowly, the specification requires knowledge and understanding of four objectives of government macroeconomic policy. These are:

- full employment (or low unemployment)
- economic growth (and higher living standards)
- control of inflation
- a satisfactory balance of payments

If all these objectives could be achieved simultaneously and all the time, the economic problem would largely disappear. However, it is very difficult and perhaps impossible to achieve this. Very often, the more successful a government is at hitting one particular objective, the poorer is its performance with regard to one or more of the other objectives. Governments are often faced with policy conflicts, which they may try to resolve by trading off between competing objectives. (A trade-off occurs when a government tries to achieve an acceptable level of performance with regard to two competing objectives, because it is difficult and perhaps impossible to achieve both fully at the same time. For example, the government might aim for a 3.0% unemployment rate and a 2.0% inflation rate, because it believes that absolute full employment and zero inflation are mutually exclusive and impossible to achieve together.)

3.2.4 Macroeconomic policy

Whereas specification section 3.2.3 covers the objectives of macroeconomic policy, this section is concerned with the types of economic policy, or policy instruments, used to try to achieve the objectives. This involves fiscal, monetary and supply-side policies.

Fiscal policy covers taxation and government spending and the government's budget deficit or surplus, while interest rates are the main monetary policy instrument. In the past, fiscal policy was mostly used to influence aggregate demand, but this is seldom the case today. Monetary policy has traditionally centred on the raising or lowering of interest rates primarily to manage aggregate demand in pursuit of the objective of controlling inflation. The specifications also require you to understand how monetary policy may affect the money supply and exchange rate, and the role of the Bank of England in implementing monetary policy.

It is now generally agreed that the success of the UK economy depends on how well the supply side of the economy performs. Consequently, much emphasis is now placed on supply-side policies. For the most part, supply-side policies are free-market and anti-interventionist and increase the economy's production potential by improving competition, the efficiency of markets and resource allocation.

You must make sure you can use the *AD/AS* macroeconomic model (explained in section 3.2.2) to illustrate, analyse and evaluate the effects of monetary, fiscal and supply-side policies.

■3.2.1 The measurement of macroeconomic performance

These notes relate to AQA specification section 3.2.1 and prepare you to answer examination questions on:

■ the objectives of government economic policy
■ macroeconomic indicators
■ uses of index numbers

> **Exam tip**
>
> Make sure you understand the difference between macroeconomics and microeconomics, and also appreciate how many macroeconomic theories have microeconomic foundations.

Essential information

The objectives of government economic policy

A **policy objective** is a target or goal that a government wishes to achieve or 'hit'. Since the Second World War, governments in mixed economies such as the UK have generally had the same broad range of objectives. These have been: economic growth, minimising unemployment, controlling inflation and achieving a stable balance of payments on current account. We shall now look at each of these in turn.

Economic growth

Economic growth is defined as the increase in the potential level of real output the economy can produce over a period of time, such as a year. Strictly, this is **long-run economic growth**, which is not the same as **short-run economic growth**. Long-run and short-run economic growth are illustrated in Figure 1. If initially the economy's **production possibility frontier** is PPF_1, short-run economic growth is shown by the movement from point C inside the frontier to point A on the frontier. Long-run economic growth is shown by the outward movement of the frontier to PPF_2. The movement from point A to point B depicts long-run economic growth. Short-run growth makes use of spare capacity and takes up the slack in the economy, whereas long-run growth increases total productive capacity.

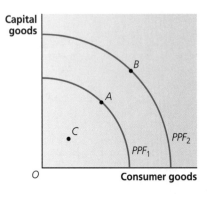

Figure 1 Economic growth illustrated by an outward movement of the economy's production possibility frontier

Policy objective A target or goal that the government's economic policy-makers wish to achieve.

Economic growth An increase in the potential output the economy can produce.

Long-run economic growth An increase in the economy's potential level of real output, and an outward movement of the economy's production possibility frontier.

Short-run economic growth Growth of real output resulting from using idle resources, including labour, thereby taking up the slack in the economy.

Production possibility frontier At the macro level, the economy's production possibility frontier shows all the different combinations of capital goods and consumer goods the economy can produce when all the factors of production are employed.

> **Knowledge check 1**
>
> How is economic growth measured for a particular year?

Economic growth generally requires the stock of physical capital (or capital goods) to grow in size and for its quality to improve. The causes of economic growth include **investment** in both physical capital, such as plant and machinery, and human capital, such as better educated and more adaptable workers, **technical progress** and growth of the working population. Net investment enlarges the stocks of physical and human capital, while technical progress leads to better quality capital replacing capital goods that have become obsolete or out of date. These also lead to higher labour productivity, which is another feature of economic growth.

Minimising unemployment

Full employment, in the sense of every economically active person in the labour force having a job, is generally impossible to achieve. As a result, economists settle for a lesser definition, for example, the level of employment at which employers' demand for labour equals the amount of labour workers are willing to supply. Nevertheless, governments wish to minimise unemployment. The appropriate policy to reduce unemployment depends on identifying correctly the underlying cause of unemployment. The different types of unemployment that the AS specification requires you to know about are seasonal unemployment, **cyclical unemployment**, **frictional unemployment** and **structural unemployment**. We explain these later in the guide in Topic 3, 'Economic performance'. A-level students must also know about voluntary and involuntary unemployment, and the natural rate of unemployment. We explain these concepts in *Student Guide 4*.

> **Frictional unemployment** occurs when a worker switches between jobs and does not immediately take up a new job.

> **Structural unemployment** Long-term unemployment occurring when some industries are declining, even though other industries may be growing. It also occurs within a growing industry if automation reduces the demand for labour, and when production requires new skills not possessed by the workers who lose their jobs.

Controlling inflation

Just as governments wish to minimise unemployment, so they aim to control the rate of inflation, though not necessarily to reduce the rate of inflation to zero. (To understand why this is generally so, see DRQ 4 on pages 85–86.) **Inflation** is defined as a persistent or continuing tendency for the price level to rise. Strictly, **deflation** is the opposite (a persistent tendency for the price level to fall), although economists often use the term to refer to the reduction in output and employment which occurs in a **recession**. When the government deflates the economy, it contracts the level of aggregate demand and economic activity. Conversely, the government expands aggregate demand to stimulate economic activity. (See Topic 4, 'Macroeconomic policy', for further information.)

Additionally, **disinflation** occurs when the rate of inflation remains positive, but slows down without falling to zero. In recent years, disinflation has been more common in the UK than a falling price level.

Investment Total planned spending by firms on capital goods produced within the economy.

Technical progress New and better ways of doing things.

Full employment Employers' demand for labour equals the amount of labour workers are willing to supply.

Cyclical unemployment Unemployment caused by a lack of aggregate demand in the economy.

Inflation A persistent and continuing tendency for the price level to rise.

Deflation A persistent and continuing tendency for the price level to fall.

Recession In the UK a recession is defined as 6 months or more (two quarters or more) of falling real GDP.

Disinflation A slowing down of a positive rate of inflation.

Stabilising the balance of payments on current account

The balance of payments measures all the currency flows into and out of an economy in a particular period of time, for example a quarter or a year. The AS Economics specification requires you to know about the current account of the balance of payments. The A-level specification also requires knowledge of capital flows, which, in the UK, figure in the financial account of the balance of payments. We explain these in *Student Guide 4*; this guide focuses only on the current account.

The current account is usually regarded as the most important part of the balance of payments because it reflects the economy's international competitiveness and the extent to which the country is living within its means. If the currency outflows in the current account exceed the currency inflows, there is a current account deficit. If receipts exceed payments, there is a current account surplus.

Macroeconomic indicators

A macroeconomic performance indicator, such as the size and rate of change of the budget deficit, provides policy-makers with information about the recent success or lack of success in achieving the target set for a particular type of economic policy such as fiscal policy. Performance indicators also provide information about whether current policy is on course to hit the future target set for the stated policy. Indicators, such as information about labour productivity and productivity gaps, can also be used to compare the performance of the UK economy with that of competitor countries.

Performance indicators can be divided into lead indicators and lag indicators:

- **Lead indicators**, such as surveys of consumer and business confidence and investment intentions, provide information about the *future* state of the economy (stemming in part from the way people are currently forming their expectations).
- **Lag indicators**, such as data on the level of GDP, and current and recent employment and unemployment figures, provide information about past and possibly current economic performance and the extent to which policy objectives such as economic growth and control of inflation have been achieved.

The usefulness of a performance indicator depends on whether it provides accurate information about the state of the economy. Performance indicators are almost always presented in the form of statistical data, for example unemployment and growth figures in the case of lag indicators, and projections about the number of house-building starts in the case of lead indicators. The accuracy of the information provided by performance indicators is thus highly dependent on the accuracy of the statistics available from the government and other sources.

Economists use lag indicator figures when measuring economic growth and when they are assessing a country's recent or current macroeconomic performance. With regard to the latter, you must always remember that the main purpose of economic activity is to improve economic welfare and people's standards of living. For the most part, this requires increased levels of consumption of material goods and services, which in turn requires the economy to produce higher levels of output or national income.

Current account of the balance of payments shows current income flows into and out of an economy, namely trade flows, investment income (primary income) and transfers (secondary income).

Performance indicator Information used to indicate how well the economy, or an aspect of the economy, is performing, e.g. trade data used to indicate the competitiveness of the country's industries.

Budget deficit occurs when government spending exceeds government revenue $(G \rightarrow T)$.

Fiscal policy Implemented in the UK by the Treasury through the use of changes in government spending, tax rates and the government's budgetary position to try to achieve policy objectives such as low unemployment.

National income The *flow* of new output produced by the economy in a particular period (e.g. a year).

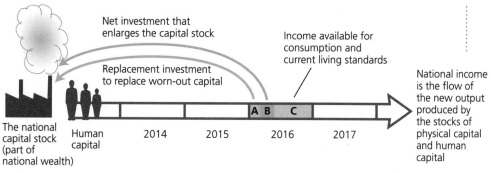

Figure 2 The production of national income

To understand national income, you must appreciate the difference between stocks and flows. There is always a national capital stock (the stock of capital goods accumulated from previous production) and a stock of human capital (the skills of the working population). These are depicted by the symbols in the left-hand part of Figure 2. National income (shown by the large arrow in Figure 2) is the flow of new output produced in a particular period (for example, 2016) by combining the economy's stocks of physical and human capital.

This flow of new output can be measured in the three ways shown in the following equation:

national output (or national product) = national income = national expenditure

'National income', 'national output' and 'national product' have exactly the same meaning, namely the flow of new goods and services produced by an economy in a particular time period, e.g. a year. Note also that national expenditure has the same value as national income and national output, being the spending of income upon the output. However, you must understand the difference between the *real* and the *nominal* values of each of the terms. Real national income (output or product) refers to the actual goods and services produced by the economy, measured in physical units such as the quantity of cars or financial services produced. By contrast, nominal national income (output or product) measures the flow of new goods and services in monetary terms, namely at the price level when the output was produced. (Nominal national income is also called money national income.)

The relationship between nominal national income and real national income is:

nominal national income = real national income × the price level

The large arrow in Figure 2 shows the flow of national income over 4 years: 2014, 2015, 2016 and 2017. When producing national income in a particular year (2016, for example), part of the national capital stock wears out. Unless worn-out capital is replaced, the national capital stock shrinks and negative economic growth is likely to occur. To prevent this, part of 2016's national income (shown by rectangle A in Figure 2) must be invested to repair or make good the size of the capital stock. Gross national income (GNI) or gross national product (GNP) refers to national income *before* deducting the amount of income invested to maintain the capital stock. Net national income (NNI) measures national income or output *after* this payment has been made. **Gross domestic product (GDP)** is similar to GNI, but measures the flow of output produced within the UK. By contrast, GNI includes profits flowing to UK companies

Gross domestic product (GDP) The sum of all goods and services, or level of output, produced in the economy over a period of time, e.g. 1 year.

from their activities overseas, while deducting profits flowing out of the UK made by overseas multinational companies from their activities in the UK.

Like national income and national output, GDP can also be measured in terms of either real GDP or nominal GDP. Consider a situation in which nominal GDP rises by 3% but the inflation rate is 5%. In this situation, *real* GDP is actually falling. And when measuring standards of living, real GDP per capita (per head of population) is a better measure of average economic welfare than 'raw' real GDP figures. For example, if the population grows by 10% while real GDP only grows by 3%, real GDP per capita falls. Finally, even if real GDP is growing, the figure takes no account of the distribution of income between rich and poor. The rich may be getting better off, while the poor become worse off.

Four other sets of data which also contribute to the measurement of economic performance are: inflation data, unemployment data, productivity data and data on the current account of the balance of payments.

Inflation

The two measures of inflation that you need to understand in some detail are the **consumer prices index (CPI)** and the **retail prices index (RPI)**. For many years, the RPI was the measure of the average price level of consumer goods and services, and was used in the UK for calculating the rate of consumer price or retail price inflation. In recent years, the CPI has replaced the RPI, not only for measuring the average price level and the rate of consumer price inflation, but also when setting the government's target rate of inflation, and for purposes such as uprating pensions and other welfare benefits, and sometimes public sector pay. (For further information about measuring inflation, see DRQ 4 on pages 85–91.

Until 2003, the rate of inflation was measured in the UK by changes in the RPI. The government still uses the RPI for this purpose, but as noted above, the CPI has now become the main measure of inflation. A price index such as the RPI or CPI attempts to measure the cost of living of a representative family in the economy. Each month, the prices of all the goods in a selected 'national shopping basket' are recorded at hundreds of shops, so that the price index for that month can be calculated. Each of the items in the shopping basket is given a weight to reflect its importance in family spending. Suppose the price index this year is 105, whereas last year (the base year) it was 100. Given these numbers, the 5-point move in the index means that the rate of inflation over the year was 5%. But if the price index numbers for the 2 years are 110 (this year) and 105 (last year), the rate of inflation is a little below 5%. Can you work out why?

Unemployment

With regard to unemployment and employment, the UK government measures unemployment in two ways. One is the **claimant count**, which simply measures the number of people claiming Jobseeker's Allowance from the government. The second method of measurement is based on the **Labour Force Survey (LFS)**. The LFS is a quarterly survey of 60,000 households, which counts people as unemployed if they are actively seeking work and have not had a job during the week in question. The LFS measure of unemployment is higher by several hundreds of thousands than the claimant count, largely because people may be actively looking for work without

Exam tip

Make sure you can interpret national income statistics, which may be included in both multiple-choice and data-response questions.

Consumer prices index (CPI) An index used to calculate the rate of consumer price inflation in the UK.

Retail prices index (RPI) An index used to calculate the rate of retail price inflation in the UK.

Claimant count The number of people registered to claim unemployment benefit.

Labour Force Survey (LFS) A quarterly sample survey of households in the UK which provides information on UK labour markets.

claiming benefits, either because they don't qualify for benefits or because they rely for income on other members of their family.

Productivity

In general terms, productivity measures output (of goods and services) per unit of input. For the most part, however, when economists mention productivity, they mean **labour productivity**. This is output per worker in a particular period of time, say 1 year. Labour productivity is one of the most important measures of macroeconomic performance. An increase in output per worker is an important cause of long-run economic growth, higher living standards and increased competitiveness of the economy in international markets. (For further mention of productivity, see Extracts A, B and C in DRQ 1 on pages 61–62.)

Current account of the balance of payments

The competitiveness of the economy in international markets is also reflected in data on the balance of payments on current account. As we said earlier in the context of a government's macroeconomic objectives, the current account reflects the economy's international competitiveness and the extent to which the country is living within its means. (For further mention of the balance of payments on current account, see DRQ 5 on pages 95–99.)

Uses of index numbers

We have already mentioned **index numbers** in the context of measuring the price level and inflation. Changes in real GDP, along with other economic variables, are usually expressed using index numbers. Economists frequently use index numbers when making comparisons over periods of time. An index starts in a given year, called the base year, which is given an index number of 100. In later years or months an increase in the size of the variable causes the index number to rise above 100, while a fall in the size of the variable, compared to the base year, results in the index number falling to below 100. For example, an index number of 105 means a 5% rise from the base year, whereas an index number of 95 means a 5% fall.

There are two points to be aware of when interpreting data expressed in index numbers:

- Providing you are comparing the index number for a particular year with the base year index number of 100, the increase in the index number is the same as the percentage increase over the data period you are looking at.
- However, as noted, when a comparison is made with a year other than the base year, a change in the value of index numbers is not the same as a percentage change over the period. In August 2015, the CPI, which measures inflation, stood at 128.4. Two years earlier in August 2013 it had been 126.4. The price level thus increased by two index points over the 2-year period. To calculate the percentage change over the 2-year period, we use the following formula:

$$\text{percentage increase} = \frac{\text{change in index points}}{\text{index number for 2013}} \times 100$$

or

$$\frac{2}{126.4} \times 100$$

which is 1.58%

Labour productivity
Output per worker in a year, quarter, month or week.

Index number A number used in an index, such as the consumer prices index, to enable accurate comparisons over time to be made. The base year index number is usually 100.

Knowledge check 4

Outline one advantage of expressing economic data in index numbers.

Exam tip

At both AS and A-level, you must be able to interpret index numbers. At A-level, you may also be asked to make calculations from data presented in the form of index numbers.

2005 was the base year for the CPI over this period, with the index standing at 100. The index point change of 28.4 index points between 2005 and August 2015 in this case led to a percentage change over the period of 28.4%.

Examination skills

The skills most likely to be tested by multiple-choice and data-response questions on the measurement of macroeconomic performance, both at AS and the full A-level, are as follows:

■ Identifying and briefly explaining the main objectives of macroeconomic policy.
■ Understanding how the importance of different policy objectives has changed over the years.
■ Comparing the performance of the UK and other countries in achieving policy objectives.
■ Understanding how inflation and unemployment are measured, and being familiar with terms such as frictional unemployment and the different causes of inflation described in this guide in Topic 3, 'Economic performance'.
■ Drawing on different forms of economic data to analyse economic issues and problems.
■ Understanding national income and measures of national income such as real GDP.

Examination questions

In AS Paper 2, you should expect up to three of the 20 multiple-choice questions to be set on the measurement of macroeconomic performance, including at least one on data interpretation. In A-level Paper 3, you should expect at least one of the 30 multiple-choice questions (covering both microeconomics and macroeconomics) to be on the measurement of macroeconomic performance. MCQ 1 on page 54 is an example of a question set on national income, economic growth and the economic cycle. MCQ 2 is testing your knowledge of unemployment and inflation. MCQ 3 requires interpretation of index numbers, a skill which is also required for DRQ 4 (page 85). DRQ 1 (pages 61–63) asks for two significant points of comparison between the changes in GDP per hour worked in the seven countries shown in the data in the questions.

Common examination errors

Commonly made mistakes on the measurement of macroeconomic performance include:

■ failure to explain the meaning of particular policy objectives, such as full employment
■ confusing policy objectives, policy instruments, and policy and performance indicators
■ not understanding national income concepts such as real GDP
■ confusing budget deficits with balance of payment deficits on current account
■ at AS, the inability to interpret index numbers, and at A-level, the additional inability to calculate index numbers

Summary

- The main objectives of government macroeconomic policy are full employment, economic growth, control of inflation and a satisfactory or sustainable balance of payments on current account, though a fair distribution of income and wealth is sometimes added to this list.
- Unemployment, which is measured by the claimant count and the LFS, divides into cyclical, frictional, structural and seasonal unemployment.

- The rate of inflation is measured by changes in the CPI and the RPI.
- Inflation should not be confused with the related concepts of deflation and disinflation.
- Economic data is often presented in the form of index numbers.
- National income concepts such as real GDP per capita must be understood.

■3.2.2 How the macroeconomy works: the circular flow of income, *AD/AS* analysis and related concepts

These notes relate to AQA AS specification section 3.2.2 and A-level specification section 4.2.2, and prepare you to answer examination questions on the following:

- the circular flow of income
- aggregate demand and aggregate supply analysis
- determinants of aggregate demand
- aggregate demand and the level of economic activity
- determinants of short-run aggregate supply
- determinants of long-run aggregate supply

Essential information

The circular flow of income

To understand the **circular flow of income**, it is first necessary to understand the meaning of **aggregate demand**. Aggregate demand, which comprises total planned spending on the real output (goods and services) that the economy produces, is represented by the following equation:

aggregate demand = consumption + investment + government spending + net exports (exports − imports)

or:

$$AD = C + I + G + (X - M)$$

where C, I, G, X and M are the symbols used respectively for **consumption**, **investment**, **government spending** and net export demand, i.e. **exports** minus **imports**.

These are known as the 'components of aggregate demand'. If the value of any of these components changes, aggregate demand also changes, either increasing or decreasing. Each of the components of aggregate demand originates in a different sector of the economy. Households are responsible for consumption, and firms for investment, while government spending and net export demand $(X - M)$ originate respectively in the government sector and the overseas sector.

A circular flow model, as illustrated in Figure 3, can be used to analyse the effects of injections of spending and withdrawals of spending on the national economy. The dashed flow lines in the diagram show the *real* flows occurring in the economy between households and firms. Households supply labour and other factor services in exchange for goods and services produced by the firms. But these real flows generate money flows (or *nominal* flows) of income and spending shown by the solid flow lines.

Circular flow of income measures how real and nominal income circulate round the economy.

Aggregate demand Total planned spending on real national output by all the economic agents in the economy in a particular time period.

Consumption Planned spending by households on consumer goods and services.

Investment Planned spending by firms on capital goods.

Government spending Planned spending by government on goods and services.

Imports Planned spending by domestic residents on overseas-produced goods and services.

Exports Planned spending by overseas residents on domestically produced goods and services.

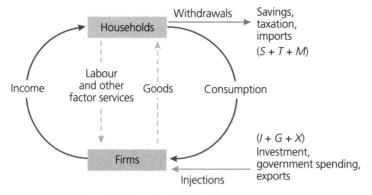

Figure 3 The circular flow of income

Suppose that all the income received by households (shown by the left-hand flow curve of the diagram) is spent on consumption (shown by the right-hand flow curve). In this situation, all the income received by households from selling their factor services to firms would recirculate back to the firms when spent on the goods and services produced by the firms. The circular flow of income would be complete. In the jargon of economics, there would be no withdrawals or leakages of spending out of the circular flow of income, but likewise, there would be no injections of spending into the circular flow.

However this is too simple. Figure 3 shows three leakages of spending out of the circular flow. These are **saving**, **taxation** and imports ($S + T + M$). These are shown by the horizontal arrow at the top of the diagram. As well as these three leakages of spending, there are three **injections** of spending into the circular flow. These are investment, government spending and exports (I, G and X). The three injections of demand are shown by the horizontal arrow at the bottom of the diagram.

If the three leakages of spending out of the circular flow of income exactly equal the three injections (i.e. if $S + T + M = I + G + X$), the economy is in a state of **macroeconomic equilibrium**. Conversely, if leakages exceed injections or vice versa, there is macroeconomic disequilibrium.

For example:

- if $S + T + M > I + G + X$, there is a net leakage of spending out of the circular flow
- if $S + T + M < I + G + X$, there is a net injection of spending into the circular flow

In the former case, unless there is an adjustment mechanism that quickly gets rid of the inequality, national income falls until, at a lower level of income, equilibrium is restored with $S + T + M = I + G + X$. In the latter case, again assuming a lack of an adjustment mechanism, national income increases until, at a higher level of income, macroeconomic equilibrium is again restored with $S + T + M = I + G + X$.

Aggregate demand and aggregate supply analysis

Along with the circular flow model of the economy explained in the previous section, the **aggregate demand and aggregate supply** (AD/AS) **macroeconomic model** provides the theoretical core of 'The national economy in a global context' specification. At the heart of the AD/AS model are two curves, the **aggregate demand** (AD) curve and the **aggregate supply** (AS) curve, which are illustrated in

Saving Income which is not consumed.

Taxation Revenue raised by government through compulsory levies on households, firms and imports.

Injections Spending which is injected into the circular flow of income.

Macroeconomic equilibrium occurs when $S + T + M = I + G + X$ in the circular flow model and when $AD = AS$ in the AD/AS model.

Knowledge check 5

Use the circular flow model to explain the difference between real and nominal flows.

Aggregate demand and aggregate supply macroeconomic model A macroeconomic model which can be used to analyse the effects on the economy of changes in aggregate demand and aggregate supply.

Aggregate demand The total planned spending on real output produced within the economy.

Aggregate supply The total real output of goods and services that firms and other producers plan to supply in a particular time period.

Figure 4. The curve drawn in Figure 4 (and also in Figure 5) is a **short-run aggregate supply** (*SRAS*) curve, which differs from the **long-run aggregate supply** (*LRAS*) curve explained later in this guide.

Aggregate demand is the sum of total planned consumption spending by households, total planned investment spending by firms, government spending on real output and the net amount spent on the economy's real output by the rest of the world (spending on exports minus spending by UK residents on imports — or net export demand). As we mentioned earlier, these items are called the components of aggregate demand.

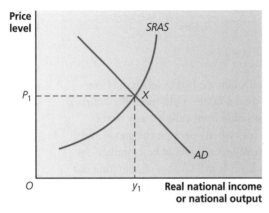

Figure 4 An aggregate demand curve, a short-run aggregate supply curve and macroeconomic equilibrium

The *AD* curve in Figure 4 slopes downwards to the right, showing that aggregate demand for goods and services rises as the average price level falls.

Just as aggregate demand comprises total planned spending on real national output that all the economic agents in the economy plan to undertake, so aggregate supply is the total output of goods and services that the firms or producers in the economy wish to supply and sell. In contrast to the negatively sloping *AD* curve in Figure 4, the *SRAS* curve, which slopes upwards to the right, shows firms responding to higher average prices by planning to supply more goods and services.

The section on circular flow theory explained how macroeconomic equilibrium occurs when leakages or withdrawals of spending from the circular flow of income equal injections of spending into the flow, i.e. when $S + T + M = I + G + X$. Macroeconomic equilibrium can also be defined as occurring at the level of real national income or output at which aggregate demand equals aggregate supply ($AD = AS$). In Figure 4, macroeconomic equilibrium occurs at point X, which is positioned above real income level y_1.

Shifts of the AD and the SRAS curves

The *position* of the *AD* curve, as distinct from the *slope* of the curve, is determined by the size of the different components of aggregate demand: C, I, G and $(X - M)$. When any of these components changes in size, the *AD* curve shifts to a new position. For example, an increase in C shifts the *AD* curve rightward.

Costs of production are the main determinant of the position of the *SRAS* curve. For example, when production costs rise, perhaps because of rising wage costs, the *SRAS* curve shifts leftward.

Short-run aggregate supply Aggregate supply when capital is fixed.

Long-run aggregate supply A measure of the total real output that can be produced when the economy is producing the normal capacity level of output.

Knowledge check 6

What is the difference between aggregate demand and national expenditure?

Knowledge check 7

What is the difference between macroeconomic equilibrium and microeconomic equilibrium?

Exam tip

Don't confuse aggregate demand with aggregate supply, or with microeconomic demand.

Figure 5 shows an upward-sloping *SRAS* curve, together with a number of *AD* curves. The position of the *AD* curves is determined by adding together all the components of aggregate demand $C + I + G + (X - M)$. As we noted earlier, if one or more of the components of aggregate demand change, the *AD* curve shifts to a new position. For example, an increase in consumption, investment or overseas demand for the country's exports shifts the *AD* curve to the right (from AD_1 to AD_2 in Figure 5), as does a fall in imports or an increase in government spending. Conversely, a decrease in C, I or X, or an increase in M, shifts the *AD* curve to the left, as does a fall in government spending.

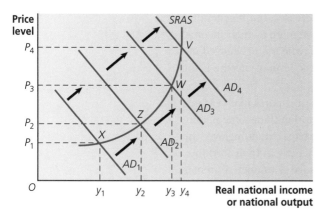

Figure 5 Using the *AD/AS* model to analyse the national economy

Figure 5 tells us that, with an upward-sloping *SRAS* curve, an increase in aggregate demand can simultaneously **reflate** real output and create jobs, and **inflate** the price level. The extent to which the demand increase is reflationary or inflationary depends on the steepness of the *SRAS* curve to the right of the initial macroeconomic equilibrium. Suppose, for example, that macroeconomic equilibrium is initially at point X in Figure 5, with the aggregate demand curve in position AD_1. In this situation, which depicts a recessionary economy suffering significant demand deficiency, an increase in aggregate demand to AD_2 increases both output and the price level. Although the increase in aggregate demand simultaneously reflates and inflates the economy, the reflationary effect is greater as long as the *SRAS* curve is gently sloped. Real output and the price level both increase, to y_2 and P_2 respectively, to bring about a new macroeconomic equilibrium at point Z.

However, as the *SRAS* curve becomes steeper, any further increase in aggregate demand, for example to AD_3, is more inflationary than reflationary. The increase in aggregate demand to AD_3 moves macroeconomic equilibrium to point W. Real output has increased to y_3, and the price level has risen to P_3. Finally, following the move from AD_3 to AD_4, the new macroeconomic equilibrium occurs at point V. The diagram tells us that any further increase in aggregate demand to the right of AD_4 solely causes inflation. The economy produces at full capacity (being on its production possibility frontier), so real output cannot increase any further, at least in the short run.

The determinants of aggregate demand

In this section, we survey the various factors which determine and affect the size of each of the components of aggregate demand: C, I, G and $(X - M)$.

Reflate The production of a higher level of real output resulting from an increase in aggregate demand.

Inflate A rising price level resulting from excess aggregate demand.

Exam tip

There are two ways of stating macroeconomic equilibrium: in the circular flow model $(S + T + M = I + G + X)$ and in the *AD/AS* model $(AD = AS)$. In an exam context, use the definition you decide is most appropriate to the question you are answering.

Knowledge check 8

What effects will a cut in the rate of income tax have on aggregate demand and aggregate supply?

Consumption

The factors that determine household consumption in the economy also determine household saving. When consumption rises, saving falls, and vice versa. The determinants of consumption (and saving) include:

- **Interest rates** The rate of interest rewards savers for sacrificing current consumption, and the higher the rate of interest, the greater the reward. Thus at any particular level of income, the amount saved increases as the real rate of interest rises and the amount spent on consumption falls.
- **The level of income** Consumption rises as income increases, but it generally rises at a slower rate than income. As a result, households save more as their incomes increase. The famous economist John Maynard Keynes, who many believed more or less invented modern macroeconomics, argued that the level of income is the most important determinant of consumption and saving.
- **Expected future income** The current level of income in a particular year may have much less influence on a person's planned consumption than some notion of expected income over a much longer time period, perhaps extending over the individual's remaining life. Many people save, especially early in their working lives, to finance house purchase, and then continue to save to finance retirement or to protect dependants against the financial problems that would result from the saver's early death. Saving undertaken over a number of years is followed in later years by dissaving, when a house is purchased or upon retirement.
- **Wealth** When household wealth increases — for example, when house prices or share prices rise — people often decide to consume more and save less. For members of households, an increase in wealth does their saving for them.
- **Consumer confidence** When consumer confidence increases, households generally spend more and save less, whereas a fall in optimism (or a growth in pessimism) has the opposite effect. This links in with the wealth effect just described. As well as becoming wealthier, owner-occupiers become more confident about the future when house prices are rising faster than general inflation. Rapidly rising house prices lead to a consumer spending spree in the shops.
- **The availability of credit** When credit becomes easy to obtain, consumption increases as people supplement current income by borrowing on credit created by the banking system.

Investment

Investment must not be confused with saving. As a general rule, households save while firms invest. Investment is defined as total planned spending by firms on capital goods, such as plant, machinery and raw materials. The determinants of investment include:

- **The rate of interest** From a firm's point of view, the rate of interest is the cost of borrowing. Firms invest more as the rate of interest falls, since it becomes cheaper to raise the funds to finance investment in new capital goods.
- **Business confidence** Investment increases as business confidence grows because entrepreneurs believe that higher profits can be made in the future.
- **Technical progress** Existing machinery will eventually become obsolete or out of date. Firms invest in new state-of-the-art plant and machinery, which replaces old capital equipment.

Rate of interest The price of borrowed money and the reward for saving.

Wealth A stock of assets.

Knowledge check 9

Distinguish between consumption, saving and investment.

Knowledge check 10

How does the rate of interest affect saving and investment?

- **The relative prices of capital and labour** When wages rise relative to the price of capital, firms tend to adopt more capital-intensive technologies, replacing labour with capital. To remind you, investment is spending on capital goods.
- **The accelerator** A firm producing at full capacity has to invest in extra capacity in order to meet higher future demand for its output. The accelerator is the number that links the change in current output to the extra capital needed to produce the additional output. For example, if the value of the accelerator is 4, one unit of extra output next year requires investment in four units of extra capital this year.

The government sector

The government sector is a source of aggregate demand in the economy (government spending) and — through taxation — the government is also responsible for a major leakage of spending out of the circular flow of income. The net effect of government spending on aggregate demand depends on the nature of the government's budget. There are three possibilities:

- A budget deficit ($G > T$), when government spending is greater than tax revenue, represents expansionary fiscal policy with the government injecting spending and demand into the economy.
- A **budget surplus** ($G < T$) is the opposite. There is a net leakage of spending out of the economy as tax revenue exceeds government spending. Fiscal policy is contractionary or deflationary.
- The government may aim for a **balanced budget** ($G = T$), which has a generally neutral effect on aggregate demand.

The overseas sector

We have explained that spending on UK exports by residents of other countries is an injection of spending into the UK economy and increases aggregate demand. Conversely, spending by UK residents on imports produced in other countries is a leakage of spending, which decreases aggregate demand. When $X > M$, the balance of payments on current account is generally in surplus. But when $X < M$, there is generally a balance of payments deficit on current account. Refer to DRQ 5 on pages 91–99 for further information on the impact of the overseas sector on the UK economy.

Aggregate demand and the level of economic activity

In our discussion of Figure 5 and of the effects of shifts of the aggregate demand curve, we explained certain aspects of how changes in aggregate demand affect the level of economic activity. In this section, we focus on a particular aspect of this relationship – the multiplier.

The national income multiplier measures the relationship between an initial change in a component of aggregate demand, such as government spending or investment, and the resulting change in the level of national income. Suppose, for example, that government spending increases by £10 billion and that households receive this sum. Most, but not all, of the £10 billion is then spent on consumption — though part of it leaks into saving, taxation and imports. The fraction spent on consumption increases shopkeepers' incomes. At the next stage, the shopkeepers spend a fraction

Accelerator A change in investment levels resulting from a change in the level of real national output.

Budget surplus occurs when government spending is less than government revenue from taxes and other sources ($G \leftarrow T$).

Balanced budget occurs when government spending equals government revenue from taxes and other sources ($G = T$).

Balance of payments deficit When earnings from exports, inward investment income and inward transfer income are less than outward spending on imports, investment and transfer income.

Multiplier Named after the increase in real national income which results from an initial change in aggregate demand.

of their extra income on consumption, which causes a further increase in consumer demand. The process continues with successive spending increases, each of which is accompanied by an equal increase in national income and output.

Because the total amount by which income and output increases is a multiple of the initial increase in spending, the process is known as the multiplier process. For example, if the size of the multiplier is 2, an initial increase in government spending of £10 billion causes national income to rise by £20 billion. To capture the flavour of the multiplier process, think of ripples spreading over a pond after throwing a stone into the water. Each of the ripples resembles a stage in the multiplier process.

The investment multiplier and the accelerator

We shall now compare the investment multiplier with the accelerator. Students often confuse the investment multiplier with the accelerator, which is mentioned in the earlier section covering the determinants of investment. The accelerator works in the opposite direction to the investment multiplier. Whereas the investment multiplier measures how a change in private sector investment induces a change in the equilibrium level of national income, which ends up as a multiple of the initial change in investment, the accelerator measures how a change in the rate of growth of national income induces a change in the level of investment.

Multiple-choice questions are used to test your understanding of the multiplier and the accelerator, and the difference between the two concepts.

Determinants of short-run aggregate supply

Economists identify two aggregate supply curves: the short-run aggregate supply (SRAS) curve and the long-run aggregate supply (LRAS) curve. We shall now explain the SRAS curve, while the final section of the topic explains the LRAS curve.

Figure 6 illustrates a SRAS curve. The curve shows that firms plan to supply more real output as the price level rises. At the average price level P_1, firms plan to supply the level of real output y_1. To persuade the firms it is in their interest to produce the larger output of y_2, the price level must rise to P_2 in order to create conditions in which profit-maximising firms are willing and able to supply more output. If prices don't rise, firms won't increase output.

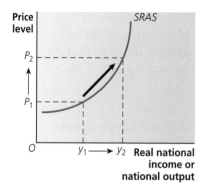

Figure 6 A short-run aggregate supply (SRAS) curve

Knowledge check 11

What is the difference between the investment multiplier and the accelerator?

Exam tip

At AS, you will not be asked to calculate the value of either the multiplier or the accelerator. However, you should understand both concepts and not confuse the two. At A-level you may be required to calculate the simple multiplier.

As with an *AD* curve, the slope of the *SRAS* curve must not be confused with a shift of the curve. The *SRAS* curve is constructed under the assumption that all the determinants of aggregate supply other than the price level remain unchanged. Should any of these determinants change, the *SRAS* curve shifts to a new position. The curve can shift either to the right (an increase in aggregate supply) or to the left (a decrease in aggregate supply).

Among the factors that cause a rightward shift of the *SRAS* curve are a fall in businesses' costs of production, a fall in taxes imposed on firms, and technical progress which improves the quality and productivity of the capital goods employed by firms.

Determinants of long-run aggregate supply

As we have just seen, in the short run, aggregate supply depends in part on the average price level in the economy. Firms are prepared to supply more output if the price level increases.

However, in the long run, aggregate supply reflects the economy's production potential, which is independent of changes in the average price level. This means that the *LRAS* curve is a vertical line, located above the economy's normal capacity level of output. This is the level of output at which the full production potential of the economy is being used, with the economy producing on its production possibility frontier.

This is illustrated in Figure 7, which shows the economy's *AD* curve shifting up the vertical *LRAS* curve. The position of the normal capacity level of output, y_N, is determined by available technology, productivity (output per worker), people's motivation to work hard and/or to be entrepreneurial, factor mobility, and the effectiveness of economic incentives and institutions such as banks in providing finance to businesses.

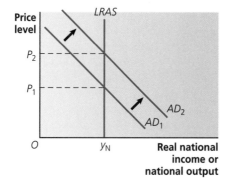

Figure 7 An economy's *AD* curve shifting up a vertical *LRAS* curve

As Figure 7 shows, once the economy produces the normal capacity level of output y_1, an increase in aggregate demand from AD_1 to AD_2 increases average prices from P_1 to P_2, but real output remains unchanged (see, however, Figure 12, page 31).

Improvement in any of the factors determining the normal capacity level of output increases the economy's ability to supply output and shifts the *LRAS* curve to the right, as shown by the movement from $LRAS_1$ to $LRAS_2$ in Figure 8. A shift to the right of the $LRAS$ curve illustrates economic growth, as does a similar shift of the economy's production possibility frontier.

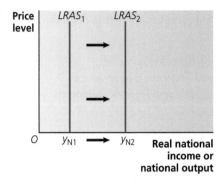

Figure 8 A rightward shift of the $LRAS$ curve

Although most economists believe that the $LRAS$ curve is vertical, some say that Keynes believed the AS curve to have a different shape, both in the short run and in the long run. This curve, shown in Figure 9, is called the **Keynesian AS curve**. As Figure 9 illustrates, the Keynesian AS curve is horizontal before becoming vertical. The horizontal section is explained by two of Keynes's assumptions about the way the economy functions.

Keynesian economists believe that because of deficient aggregate demand, an economy can settle into a long-run equilibrium known as an under-full employment equilibrium (e.g. y_1 in this diagram). Because there is spare capacity, an increase in AD causes real output to increase, but not the price level.

However, once change to a high level of employment has been reached, at y_N, the Keynesian AS curve takes on the properties of the vertical $LRAS$ curve. If aggregate demand increases, only the price level, and not real output, increases. This is because the economy is now producing at full capacity.

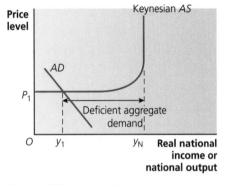

Figure 9 The Keynesian AS curve

Keynesian AS curve A reverse 'L'-shaped AS curve associated with the economist John Maynard Keynes.

Exam tip

The AS specification advises that the $LRAS$ curve should be assumed to be vertical, but the A-level specification requires knowledge of the Keynesian AS curve as well as the vertical $LRAS$ curve.

Examination skills

The skills most likely to be tested by multiple-choice and data-response questions on how the macroeconomy works: the circular flow of income, aggregate demand/ aggregate supply analysis and related concepts, are as follows:

- Ability to draw accurately both circular flow and *AD/AS* diagrams.
- Explaining and analysing economic issues and problems with the help of *AD/AS* diagrams.
- Understanding the meaning of aggregate demand and the components of aggregate demand.
- Explaining two or three of the determinants of consumption (and/or saving).
- Explaining two or three of the determinants of investment.
- Interpreting a circular flow diagram in a multiple-choice question.
- Using a circular flow diagram to explain how a change in a component of aggregate demand may affect the economy.
- Defining the multiplier and the accelerator and explaining both processes.

Examination questions

In AS Paper 2, you should expect up to three of the 20 multiple-choice questions to be set on how the macroeconomy works: the circular flow of income, aggregate demand/aggregate supply analysis and related concepts. In A-level Paper 3, you should expect at least one of the 30 multiple-choice questions (covering both microeconomics and macroeconomics) to be on this topic. MCQ 4 on pages 85–91 is an example of a question on the circular flow of income. MCQ 5 is about the multiplier and the accelerator. MCQ 6 is testing your knowledge of the *AD/AS* macroeconomic model. DRQs 1 (pages 61–63) and 4 (page 85) ask you to apply *AD/AS* analysis to how a fall in investment might affect real national output and the price level, and to how a 'bad' deflation is caused.

Common examination errors

Commonly made mistakes on how the macroeconomy works: the circular flow of income, aggregate demand/aggregate supply analysis and related concepts include the following:

- inaccurate drawing of circular flow and *AD/AS* diagrams
- confusing *AD* and *AS* curves
- confusing short-run and long-run aggregate supply curves (*SRAS* and *LRAS*)
- mislabelling the axes of *AD/AS* diagrams (e.g. writing 'inflation' instead of 'price level' on the vertical axis, or 'employment' rather than 'national output' or 'real output' on the horizontal axis)
- failure to identify the factors that can lead to shifts of the *AD* curve and/or the *AS* curve
- confusing macroeconomic *AD/AS* diagrams with microeconomic supply and demand diagrams

Content Guidance

Summary

- The circular flow model and the *AD/AS* macroeconomic model provide the theoretical frameworks you are expected to use when answering data-response questions on 'The national economy in a global context'.
- A circular flow diagram shows leakages of spending from, and injections of demand into, the flows of income and spending circulating round the economy.
- Saving, taxation and imports $(S + T + M)$ are the three leakages of the flow of income.
- Investment, government spending and exports $(I + G + X)$ are the three injections into the flow of income.
- In the circular flow model, macroeconomic equilibrium occurs when $S + T + M = I + G + X$.
- In the *AD/AS* model, macroeconomic equilibrium occurs when $AD = AS$.
- The *AD* curve slopes downwards to the right, showing that aggregate demand for real output increases the lower the price level.
- The position of the *AD* curve is determined by the size of the components of aggregate demand. If any changes in size, the *AD* curve shifts to a new position.
- The components of aggregate demand are consumption, investment, government spending and net export demand $AD = C + I + G + (X - M)$.
- The *SRAS* curve slopes upwards to the right, showing that aggregate supply of real output increases the higher the price level.
- The position of the *SRAS* curve is largely determined by costs of production. If costs of production change, the *SRAS* curve shifts to a new position.
- The *LRAS* curve is vertical and located at the full-employment level of real output. The economy is producing at full potential.
- The *LRAS* curve shifts to the right if potential output increases, with the economy's production possibility frontier shifting outwards. A rightward shift of the *LRAS* curve shows long-run economic growth taking place.
- Improvements in technology, productivity, motivation, entrepreneurial and labour market incentives, and factor mobility can all shift the *LRAS* curve rightward, as can an improvement in the institutional set-up of the economy.

■3.2.3 Economic performance

These notes relate to AQA AS specification section 3.2.3 and to parts of A-level specification 4.2.3 and prepare you to answer examination questions on:

- economic growth and the economic cycle
- employment and unemployment
- inflation and deflation
- the balance of payments on current account
- possible conflicts between macroeconomic objectives
- the resulting possible policy trade-offs

Essential information

Economic growth and the economic cycle

We defined economic growth in the earlier topic 'The measurement of macroeconomic performance' as the increase in the potential level of *real* output that the economy can produce over a period of time, such as a year. We went on to say that this is *long-run* economic growth, which is not the same as *short-run* economic growth. Long-run and short-run economic growth were illustrated in Figure 1 on page 10. To remind you, if initially the economy's production possibility frontier is PPF_1, short-run economic growth is shown by the movement from point C inside the frontier to point A on the frontier. Long-run economic growth is shown by the outward movement of the frontier to PPF_2. The movement from point A to point B depicts long-run economic growth. Short-run growth makes use of spare capacity and takes up the slack in the economy, whereas long-run growth increases total productive capacity.

Economic growth generally requires the stock of physical capital (or capital goods) to grow in size and for its quality to improve. The causes of economic growth include:

- investment in both physical capital, such as plant and machinery, and human capital, such as better educated and more adaptable workers
- technical progress
- growth of the working population

Net investment enlarges the stocks of physical and human capital, while technical progress leads to better quality capital replacing capital goods that have become obsolete or out of date. These also lead to higher labour productivity, which is another feature of economic growth.

Actual growth and the economic cycle

As well as distinguishing between long-run and short-run economic growth, it is important to understand the difference between long-run or **trend growth** and **actual growth**.

- **Trend growth** The rate at which output can grow, on a sustained basis, without putting upward or downward pressure on inflation. It reflects the annual average percentage increase in the productive capacity of the economy.
- **Actual growth** The rate of growth measured at a particular point in time.

Net investment
Investment in new capital goods which adds to the national capital stock and leads to long-term economic growth.

Exam tip

Productivity is one of the most important concepts you need to know for the Paper 2 exam at AS, and for Papers 2 and 3 at A-level. It is especially important for understanding supply-side economics (see pages 47–50).

Content Guidance

Long-run or trend growth is shown in Figure 10 by the rise from year to year in the smooth trend output line. However, the economy seldom grows smoothly in this way. Instead, the rate of economic growth fluctuates from year to year, as depicted by changes in the wavy line in the diagram. The wavy line, which shows changes in actual output from year to year, illustrates the different phases of the economic cycle.

As Figure 10 shows, actual growth, which is simply the growth rate measured over the course of a particular 12-month period, may be negative as well as positive. In the UK, a **recession**, such as the one that began in 2008, occurs if real GDP falls for a period of 6 months or more. The recession ends in the trough of the economic cycle, which is followed by a recovery period and then possibly a boom.

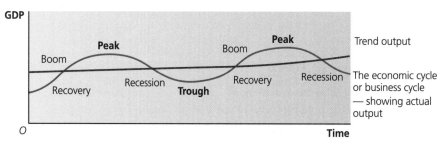

Figure 10 The phases of the economic cycle

In the context of the performance of the UK economy since 1992, Figure 10 is somewhat misleading. Over the 16-year period from 1992 to 2008, the UK enjoyed continuous economic growth and there were no recessions. (However, a severe recession began in 2008 and continued through most of 2009.) In the downturn of economic cycles between 1993 and 2008, economic growth slowed down but remained positive. During this period, and because negative economic growth did not occur, the UK government decided to mark the beginning and end of an **economic cycle** by using the concept of an **output gap**. An output gap is defined as the difference between the actual level of real output at a particular point in time and the level of output the economy would be producing had it grown continuously along the long-run growth rate, as shown by the smooth trend-growth line in Figures 10 and 11.

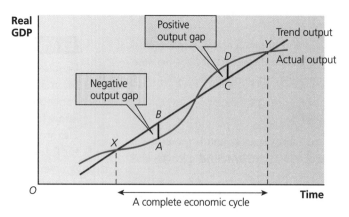

Figure 11 Output gaps and the economic cycle

Recession A fall in real output or negative economic growth for 6 months or more.

Knowledge check 12

What other names are used for the economic cycle?

Economic cycle Upswing and downswing in aggregate economic activity taking place over 4 to 12 years. Also known as a business cycle or a trade cycle.

Output gap The level of actual real output in the economy above or below the trend output level.

A complete economic cycle is now defined as the period between two dates when the economy is judged to be on trend, when the output gap is zero. A full economic cycle includes both a period in which output is below trend (with a **negative output gap**) and a period in which it is above trend (with a **positive output gap**).

A negative output gap, shown by the distance from A to B in Figure 11, occurs when actual output is below the trend output line. By contrast, a positive output gap, shown by the distance from C to D, occurs when actual output is above the trend output line. In Figure 11, points X and Y mark the beginning and end of a complete economic cycle.

Figure 12 illustrates another way of showing positive and negative output gaps on a diagram, in this case an AD/AS diagram.

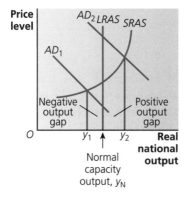

Figure 12 Positive and negative output gaps shown on an AD/AS diagram

To make sense of Figure 12 — and also economic cycle diagrams such as the ones in Figures 10 and 11, you must understand that the economy can produce *temporarily* a level of real output which is greater than potential output. Note that the $SRAS$ curve in Figure 12 continues to the right of the $LRAS$ curve and the normal capacity level of output (shown below the $LRAS$ curve). On the diagram, a negative output gap is shown by the horizontal distance between y_1 and the normal capacity level of output, and a positive output gap is shown by the horizontal distance between the normal capacity level of output and y_2.

Employment and unemployment

Full employment occurs in the economy's aggregate labour market when the aggregate demand for labour equals the aggregate supply of labour. In Figure 13, the downward-sloping aggregate demand curve for labour (AD_L) shows that as the real wage rate paid to workers falls, employers or entrepreneurs are willing to employ more labour. By contrast, the aggregate supply curve of labour in Figure 13 (AS_L) slopes upward, showing that workers supply more labour as the real wage rate rises. Full employment occurs at E_{FE}, at the market-clearing real wage rate of W_{FE}.

Types of unemployment

There are a number of different types and causes of unemployment. The ones we explain here are cyclical, frictional, seasonal and structural unemployment.

Negative output gap
The level of actual real output in the economy is lower than the trend output level.

Positive output gap
The level of actual real output in the economy is greater than the trend output level.

Full employment occurs when the aggregate demand for labour equals the aggregate supply of labour.

Exam tip

Make sure you don't confuse a standard AD/AS diagram, which shows the aggregate demand for and the aggregate supply of real *output*, with a diagram such as Figure 13, which shows the aggregate demand for and the aggregate supply of *labour* in the economy's aggregate *labour market*.

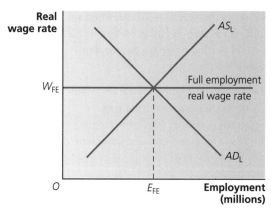

Figure 13 Full employment illustrated in the economy's aggregate labour market

Cyclical unemployment

Cyclical unemployment, which occurs in the downturn of the economic cycle, is also known as **demand-deficient unemployment** or **Keynesian unemployment**. The latter name reflects the fact that way back in the 1920s and 1930s, the great economist John Maynard Keynes identified demand deficiency as an important possible cause of unemployment in the Great Depression which occurred in a large number of the world's economies.

Figure 14 uses an *AD/AS* diagram to illustrate cyclical unemployment. In the diagram, macroeconomic equilibrium initially occurs at point *X*, immediately above y_N, which is the 'normal capacity' level of output. We shall assume that this is also the full employment level of output, which means that there is no demand deficiency in the economy. Suppose now that a collapse of consumer confidence and/or of business confidence occurs. The *AD* curve shifts to the left from AD_1 to AD_2. One of two things may now happen. In the first place, wage rates and prices may be 'sticky' or inflexible. Given this Keynesian assumption, the level of real output falls to y_2. Fewer workers are now required to produce this output. This leads to significant demand-deficient or cyclical unemployment. Alternatively, if wages and prices are flexible — as supply-side economists argue — the price level falls to bring about a new macroeconomic equilibrium at point Z. Output has still fallen, so there will still be some demand-deficient unemployment. (However, although this is not shown on the diagram, lower business costs might shift the *SRAS* curve to the right. If this happens — as supply-side anti-Keynesian economists argue — the market mechanism may eliminate the cyclical unemployment. It won't persist.)

A production possibility curve diagram, such as that drawn in Figure 15, can also be used to depict cyclical unemployment. As in Figure 1 on page 10, the economy's production possibility frontier is labelled *PPF*. Full employment occurs at all points *on* the frontier such as *A* and *B*. However, any point *inside* the frontier, such as *C*, depicts a situation in which workers are unemployed because there is insufficient demand for the output they could produce. According to Keynesian economists, aggregate demand has to rise to eliminate demand deficiency and bring about full employment at a point such as *A* or *B*. And as we explained earlier, in this situation increasing aggregate demand triggers short-term economic growth.

Demand-deficient unemployment Unemployment caused by deficient aggregate demand. Also known as cyclical unemployment and Keynesian unemployment.

Keynesian unemployment Named after the economist Keynes, this is also known as cyclical unemployment and demand-deficient unemployment. Caused by deficient aggregate demand.

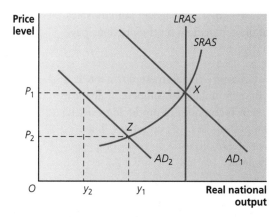

Figure 14 Using an *AD/AS* diagram to illustrate cyclical unemployment

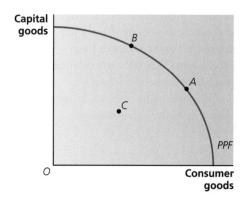

Figure 15 Using a production possibility diagram to illustrate cyclical unemployment

Frictional unemployment

Change is constantly taking place in a dynamic economy, with some industries declining and others growing. As new products are developed, and demand and cost conditions change, firms demand more of some labour skills while the demand for other types of labour declines. Economists use the terms 'frictional unemployment' and 'structural unemployment' to describe the resulting unemployment.

Frictional unemployment, as its name suggests, results from frictions in the labour market which create a delay or time lag during which a worker is unemployed when moving from one job to another. Note that our definition of frictional unemployment assumes that a job vacancy exists and that a friction in the job market, caused by either the geographical or occupational immobility of labour, prevents an unemployed worker from filling the vacancy. It follows that the number of unfilled job vacancies that exist can be used as an indicator of the level of frictional unemployment in the economy.

Seasonal unemployment

Seasonal unemployment, which is a form of casual unemployment, is a special case of frictional unemployment. It is unemployment caused by factors such as the weather and by fluctuations in seasonal demand, for example when temporary workers taken on by retailers to meet demand before Christmas are laid off during the January sales when demand slackens off. We explain frictional unemployment on the previous page.

Structural unemployment

Structural unemployment is generally more severe than frictional unemployment. It results from the structural decline of industries that are unable to compete or adapt in the face of changing demand and new products, new techniques of producing existing products and the emergence of more efficient competitors in other countries. The growth of international competition and the effect of globalisation on the economy have contributed recently to structural unemployment.

Technological unemployment can be regarded as a special case of structural unemployment, which results from the successful growth of new industries using labour-saving technology such as automation.

Inflation and deflation

Inflation is defined as a persistent or continuing tendency for the price level to rise. Strictly, as we first noted on page 11, deflation is the opposite (a persistent tendency for the price level to fall), although economists often use the word to refer to the reduction in output and employment that occurs in recessions. When the government deflates the economy, it uses the contractionary economic policies we explain in Topic 4, 'Macroeconomic policy', to reduce the level of demand and economic activity. Conversely, the government reflates the economy when it uses the expansionary policy we again explain in Topic 4.

Causes of inflation

Economists identify two types of inflation, caused respectively by events taking place on the demand side and the supply side of the economy. The two types of inflation are called demand-pull inflation and cost-push inflation.

Demand-pull inflation

When there is plenty of spare capacity in the economy, an increase in aggregate demand leads to an increase in real output and employment (reflation), rather than to an increase in the price level (inflation). However, as the level of real output gets close to the normal capacity level of output, located on an *AD/AS* graph immediately below the *LRAS* curve, reflation of real output gives way to inflation of the price level. If, for example, unemployment in the economy is incorrectly diagnosed in terms of demand deficiency (when the true cause is structural), an expansionary policy aimed at increasing aggregate demand creates excess demand. Too much demand pulls up the price level, with little or no lasting beneficial effect on employment. This is demand-pull inflation. The demand-pull theory of inflation is generally favoured by free-market and monetarist economists. In the monetarist theory of demand-pull inflation, the excess demand which pulls up the price level is blamed on an excess rate of growth of the money supply.

Cost-push inflation

By contrast, over the years many Keynesian economists have favoured the cost-push theory of inflation. To begin with, cost-push inflation was generally associated with trade unions using their monopoly power over the supply of labour to bargain for

Technological unemployment A form of structural unemployment caused by changing technology.

Knowledge check 13

Distinguish between frictional and structural unemployment.

Exam tip

Students often confuse disinflation and deflation. As mentioned both here and in Topic 1, when disinflation is taking place, the price level still rises, but the rate of inflation slows down.

Demand-pull inflation Inflation caused by excess aggregate demand.

Cost-push inflation Inflation caused by rising costs of production.

Money supply The *stock* of money in the economy at a particular point in time.

wage increases in excess of any rise in labour productivity. Keynesians argued that firms with monopoly power were prepared to pay these wage increases because they could pass on the increasing costs as price rises. From the 1960s until quite recently, trade union militancy and big business were believed to be responsible for cost-push inflation.

Imported cost-push inflation

It is now widely believed, however, that recent cost-push inflation has resulted not from excessive wage costs, but from the rising price of imports of food, raw materials or commodities and energy. Indeed, China recently began to increase the prices of the manufactured goods it exports (though it has countered this by trying to engineer a fall in the exchange rate). This has been another source of imported cost-push inflation.

The two panels of Figure 16 illustrate demand-pull and cost-push inflation. Figure 16(a) shows the average price level rising from P_1 to P_2, following a shift to the right of the AD curve from AD_1 to AD_2. The graph illustrates demand-pull inflation. Figure 16(b), by contrast, illustrates cost-push inflation. Rising business costs, such as wages, raw material and energy costs, shift the $SRAS$ curve upward and to the left from $SRAS_1$ to $SRAS_2$. Rising production costs push up the price level from P_1 to P_2.

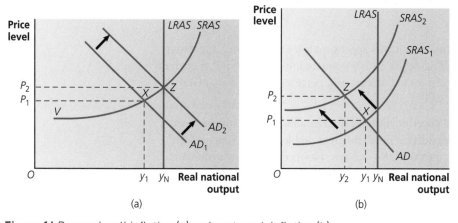

Figure 16 Demand-pull inflation (a) and cost-push inflation (b)

The leftward shift of the $SRAS$ curve that causes cost-push inflation also causes real output to fall from y_1 to y_2. The combination of a rising price level with falling or stagnant output is called **stagflation**.

Stagflation Stagnant output combined with inflation.

The balance of payments on current account

The **balance of payments accounts** are the official record published by the government of all the currency flows into and out of the country. There are two main parts to the balance of payments: the current account (see pages 12 and 15) and capital flows. The current account, which includes exports and imports, is so called because it measures income generated in the year in question flowing into and out of the economy.

Balance of payments accounts Transfers in the current account of the balance of payments.

By contrast, capital flows occur when residents of one country acquire capital assets, such as factories and oil refineries, located in other countries. Capital flows are solely an A-level topic and are explained in *Study Guide 4* rather than in this guide. Nevertheless, it is worth knowing that the acquisition of overseas-located assets leads to inward investment income (a current account item) flowing into the country in future years, and that likewise the acquisition of UK-located assets by foreign multinational companies leads to an investment income outflow. Inward and outward capital flows also affect **monetary policy**. (See *Study Guide 4* for further information about capital flows.)

Table 1 shows the first estimate of the UK's current account for 2014, published by the Office for National Statistics (ONS) in March 2015. (In later publications, it is likely that the figures will change, as the ONS regularly revises its data as more information comes to hand.)

Table 1

Items in the current account, 2014 (£ millions)	
Balance of trade in goods	−119,605
Balance of trade in services	+ 85,863
Primary income flows (Net income flows)	−38,754
Secondary income flows (Net current transfers)	−25,424
Balance of payments on the current account	**−97,920**

Source: United Kingdom Quarterly Accounts, Quarter 1 2015, ONS

In 2014, the UK's current account deficit was approximately £97.9 billion, up from a deficit of £76.7 billion in 2013. The deficit in 2014 equated to 5.5% of GDP at current market prices. This was the largest annual deficit as a percentage of nominal GDP since annual records began in 1948.

The figures suggest that the UK government has failed to stabilise the current account, though some would argue that the deficit poses no great problem if it is financed by inward capital investment flows into the UK economy. However, the chief economist at the ONS said that the current account deficit has been driven mainly by a net fall in income flowing into and out of the UK from investments earned abroad (now called **primary income**), rather than from a deteriorating net trade position. In many previous years, the UK had enjoyed a substantial surplus of investment income. The consensus view among economists is that the size of the current account deficit is unlikely to cause a crisis in the near term, but is 'storing up big problems for the future'.

Current account surpluses, deficits and equilibrium

Very often, when dealing with the current account of the balance of payments, economists simplify and pretend that there are only two items in the current account: exports and imports of goods and services (X and M). There are then three possibilities:

1 When the value of exports exceeds the value of imports (i.e. when $X > M$), there is a current account surplus.

2 When the value of exports is less than the value of imports (i.e. when $X < M$), there is a current account deficit.

3 And finally, when the value of exports equals the value of imports (i.e. when $X = M$), there is a state of current account equilibrium. (Note that the current account is in disequilibrium when there is a significant surplus or a deficit.)

Monetary policy
Uses monetary instruments such as changes in Bank Rate to try to achieve the government's monetary policy objectives such as control of inflation.

Primary income Mostly investment income flows in the current account of the balance of payments.

The different items in the current account of the balance of payments

Exports and imports

Exports and imports, which are the two main items in the current account, can be divided into exports and imports of goods (which make up the **balance of trade in goods**), and exports and imports of services (which form the **balance of trade in services**). The overall balance of trade is the sum of the balance of trade in goods and the balance of trade in services.

Primary and secondary income

The two other items in the current account that you need to understand are net primary income and net **secondary income**. These are both non-trade items in the current account.

- Net primary income, mostly investment income, includes profits flowing to UK companies from their investments in other countries, minus net profit outflows repatriated to foreign companies from their investment in the UK. Also included are net interest payments, comprising interest received by British banks on loans they have granted overseas, minus interest payments flowing to overseas banks from their loans to clients in the UK.

- Net secondary income flows or transfer flows form the second non-trade item in the current account. Examples of outward transfers from the UK are UK foreign aid and income sent overseas by immigrant workers in the UK to their families living in their countries of origin. An inward transfer would be money paid by overseas governments for the upkeep of their embassies in the UK.

Strengths and weaknesses in the UK current account

For most of recent history, the UK's current account has been in a substantial deficit. Although the balance of trade in services has been in surplus, this has been insufficient to offset a larger deficit in the balance of trade in goods.

The surplus in the balance of trade in services has resulted from the competitiveness of the City of London in world financial markets. This strength can also be viewed as a weakness, in that financial services grew at the expense of manufacturing, reflecting 'unbalance' in the UK economy. Indeed, a main weakness in the UK's current account has lain in the uncompetitiveness of UK manufactured goods in world markets. Through a process known as deindustrialisation, manufactured goods now account for less than 13% of UK output and most manufactured goods are now imported.

However, as we have noted, the primary account in the UK's current account has moved from surplus into deficit. The recent decline in the primary balance has been partly driven by a falling direct investment income balance.

The 'credit crunch', which hit world financial markets in 2007 and 2008, had an adverse effect on the export of UK financial services and illustrated a state of 'unbalance' in the UK economy. Another weakness is in the energy sector. The UK has switched in recent years from being a net exporter of oil and gas to become a net importer in a world in which energy prices have fluctuated and supplies can no longer

Balance of trade in goods The part of the current account measuring payments for exports and imports of goods.

Balance of trade in services The part of the current account measuring payments for exports and imports of services.

Secondary income Transfer flows in the current account of the balance of payments.

be guaranteed. Some economists also believe that the UK's large current account deficit imposes a significant constraint on the freedom of the UK government to pursue domestic economic policy.

Conflicts between policy objectives and trade-offs

In the past, many economists believed that because policy objectives are mutually exclusive, it is generally impossible to achieve all the objectives at the same time. A **policy conflict** exists when it is impossible to achieve two or more objectives at the same time. The government attempts to resolve this conflict by achieving a relatively satisfactory performance with regard to the conflicting objectives, or it may switch periodically from one objective to another, for example accepting higher unemployment and lower growth (for a time) in order to reduce inflation or improve the balance of payments.

Over the years, UK macroeconomic policy has been influenced and constrained by three significant policy conflicts and **policy trade-offs**:

1 There is a conflict between the *internal* policy objectives of full employment and growth and the *external* objective of achieving a satisfactory balance of payments (or possibly supporting a particular **exchange rate**).

2 There is the conflict between achieving full employment and controlling inflation. This is often called the Phillips curve trade-off. (The Phillips curve, which is explained in *Student Guide 4*, is in the A-level specification but not in the AS specification.)

3 There is a conflict between achieving economic growth together with a more equal distribution of income and wealth. During the Keynesian era, economists recommended that taxation and **transfers** to the poor should be used to reduce inequalities between rich and poor. In recent years, free-market supply-side economists have argued that such policies reduce entrepreneurial incentives and personal incentives in the labour market, inhibit growth and make the economy less competitive. In the free-market view, greater inequalities may be necessary to create the labour and entrepreneurial incentives deemed necessary for rapid and sustainable economic growth.

Exam tip

Conflicts between macroeconomic objectives have sometimes appeared to be resolved. From 1993 to 2008, UK governments were successful in achieving low unemployment, economic growth and control of inflation, though policy on improving equality and reducing the balance of payments deficit was less successful.

Knowledge check 14

State the different ways in which a budget deficit and a balance of payments deficit affect aggregate demand.

Policy conflict occurs when two or more policy objectives are mutually exclusive.

Policy trade-off The extent to which one policy objective has to be sacrificed in order to achieve another objective.

Exchange rate The external price of a currency in terms of another currency such as the US dollar or the euro.

Transfer The redistribution of income to different income groups which is not related to their production of goods or services.

Knowledge check 15

What is the difference between a policy conflict and a policy trade-off?

Examination skills

The skills most likely to be tested by multiple-choice and data-response questions on economic performance are as follows:

■ Explaining employment in terms of the demand for, and supply of, labour.
■ Relating the growth of employment to the growth of national income and output, and the resulting job creation.
■ Defining and illustrating full employment in terms of a labour market supply and demand diagram, such as Figure 13.
■ Explaining cyclical, frictional, seasonal and structural unemployment.
■ Understanding how unemployment is measured in the UK.
■ Explaining the meaning of inflation and related terms such as deflation and reflation.
■ Analysing inflation in terms of the two main theories of inflation: demand-pull and cost-push.
■ Understanding the policy conflict between low unemployment and low inflation.
■ Appreciating the relationships between the different parts of the balance of payments on current account.

Examination questions

In AS Paper 2, you should expect up to three of the 20 multiple-choice questions to be set on economic performance. In A-level Paper 3, you should expect at least one of the 30 multiple-choice questions (covering both microeconomics and macroeconomics) to be on this topic. MCQs 7, 8 and 9 on pages 56–57 focus on aspects of economic performance. All the DRQs in the Questions & Answers section of this guide also relate to economic performance.

Common examination errors

Commonly made mistakes on economic performance are:

■ lack of knowledge and understanding of the performance of the UK economy over the 10 years or so before the examination
■ an inability to compare and interpret data relating to the UK economy and similar economies, such as France and Germany
■ an inability to detect important features of data such as the economic cycle
■ failure to apply general economic knowledge to help interpret data about national economic performance
■ a tendency to assume the future will always be a continuation of the present
■ the use of words such as 'vast' and 'massive' to describe quite small changes in national economic performance
■ confusing data about national economic performance presented in index number form with percentage data
■ failure to see the connections between different indicators of national economic performance

Content Guidance

Summary

- Economic growth generally requires the stock of physical capital (or capital goods) to grow in size and for its quality to improve.
- The causes of economic growth include investment in both physical capital, such as plant and machinery, and human capital, such as better educated and more adaptable workers, technical progress and growth of the working population.
- Technical progress leads to better quality capital replacing capital goods that have become obsolete or out of date.
- Trend growth is the rate of growth in an economy averaged over a long period of years.
- Actual growth shows how the level of output fluctuates in the different phases of the economic cycle.
- A recession occurs if real GDP falls for a period of 6 months or more.
- An output gap is defined as the difference between the actual level of real output at a particular point in time and the level of output the economy would be producing had it grown continuously along its trend output line.
- Full employment occurs in the economy's aggregate labour market when the aggregate demand for labour equals the aggregate supply of labour.
- There are a number of different types and causes of unemployment, which include seasonal, cyclical, frictional and structural unemployment.
- Inflation is a persistent or continuing tendency for the price level to rise and deflation is a persistent tendency for the price level to fall.
- There are two main types of inflation: demand-pull and cost-push.
- The balance of payments comprises two main parts: the current account and capital flows.
- Exports and imports, which are the two main items in the current account of the balance of payments, divide into the balance of trade in goods and the balance of trade in services.
- The overall balance of trade is the sum of the balance of trade in goods and the balance of trade in services.
- The recent decline in the primary balance within the current account has been partly driven by a falling direct investment income balance.
- A policy conflict exists when it is impossible to achieve two or more objectives at the same time.
- Over the years, UK macroeconomic policy has been influenced and constrained by three significant policy conflicts and policy trade-offs.

■ 3.2.4 Macroeconomic policy

These notes relate to AQA AS specification section 3.2.4 and to parts of A-level specifications 4.2.4 and 4.2.5, and prepare you to answer examination questions on:

- monetary policy
- fiscal policy
- supply-side policies

Essential information

Macroeconomic policy is the part of the government's overall economic policy in which it tries to use monetary, fiscal and supply-side policy instruments to achieve the policy objectives we outlined in earlier topics. In this final topic, we explain the meanings of monetary policy (see page 36), fiscal policy (see page 12) and **supply-side policies**.

> **Macroeconomic policy** Government policy aimed at achieving macroeconomic policy objectives such as economic growth, control of inflation and low unemployment.

> **Supply-side policies** aim to improve national economic performance by creating competitive and more efficient markets, and also through interventionist policies such as government finance of labour retraining schemes.

Monetary policy

Monetary policy is any deliberate action undertaken by the government or its agents, such as the country's **central bank**, to achieve economic objectives by using monetary instruments such as **Bank Rate**, **quantitative easing** and controls over bank lending.

Until 1997, UK monetary policy was implemented more or less jointly by the Treasury (the government's finance ministry) and the central bank, the **Bank of England**. In 1997, the Bank of England was made independent and it is now the sole monetary authority, with a duty to achieve the monetary policy target set by the Treasury.

The instruments of monetary policy

In the past, controls over bank lending and controlling the growth of the money supply were used as monetary policy instruments. These days, monetary policy operates mostly through Bank Rate, which the Bank of England's **Monetary Policy Committee (MPC)** sets each month. A change in Bank Rate quickly affects other short-term interest rates (such as the overdraft rates that banks charge to personal and business customers), and usually affects mortgage interest rates at which homeowners borrow over the long term. For a short period from March 2009 until the end of October in 2012, and in response to the collapse of aggregate demand in the recession which started in 2008, a monetary policy instrument known as quantitative easing (QE) supplemented Bank Rate policy in UK monetary policy. By increasing the money supply, QE increased aggregate demand, but mostly the demand for financial assets

Central bank Controls the banking system and implements monetary policy on behalf of the government.

Bank Rate The rate of interest the Bank of England pays to commercial banks on their deposits held at the Bank of England. Bank Rate is the key policy instrument in 'conventional' monetary policy.

Quantitative easing A monetary policy instrument which, by purchasing financial assets on the open market, increases the supply of money in the economy. Sometimes called 'unconventional' monetary policy.

Bank of England The UK's central bank, which implements UK monetary policy.

Monetary Policy Committee (MPC) A group of nine people who meet at the Bank of England each month to set Bank Rate. The Committee comprises four Bank of England officials, four external appointees and the Governor of the Bank of England, who chairs the meetings.

and houses. As a result, QE led to bubbles in share and property markets, but it had much less effect on consumption and investment in the so-called real economy.

The objectives of monetary policy

By raising or lowering its own interest rate, Bank Rate (or indeed by leaving Bank Rate unchanged), the Bank of England hopes to influence the interest rates set by commercial banks, and thereby to manage the level of aggregate demand. This is done to try and achieve the policy objective set by the government, such as the control of inflation.

Prior to May 1997, monetary policy was concerned only with getting the inflation rate at or below the target rate set by the Treasury. The inflation rate target is currently 2.0%, measured by the consumer prices index (CPI). Critics argued that the policy had a built-in deflationary bias. This is no longer the case, because the MPC has in fact reduced Bank Rate to stimulate output and employment. (Indeed, from March 2009 until the time of writing this guide in January 2016, Bank Rate has remained at its lowest-ever level at 0.5%.) The Bank has believed that if the inflation rate falls below 2.0%, the fall in inflation will be accompanied by an undesirable fall in output and employment. In the words of the Labour government in power before 2010: 'The primary objective of monetary policy is price stability. But subject to that, the Bank of England must also support the government's economic policy objectives, including those for growth and employment.'

Using AD/AS diagrams to show how monetary policy affects the price level and real output

Before the short period from 2008 until 2010 when, in the fiscal stimulus, fiscal policy was used to stimulate spending in the economy, monetary policy rather than fiscal policy was used to manage the level of aggregate demand in the economy. Since 2010, once again monetary rather than fiscal policy manages aggregate demand. To understand how monetary policy is used in this way, it is worth repeating the aggregate demand equation:

$$AD = C + I + G + (X - M)$$

When people are encouraged to save, they have less income available for consumption. Higher interest rates also cause businesses to postpone or cancel investment projects because they believe that higher borrowing costs make the purchase of capital goods unprofitable. Figure 17 illustrates the effects of such a contractionary monetary policy on the price level and on real national income or output. An expansionary monetary policy, by contrast, would shift the AD curve to the right.

Linking monetary policy to the exchange rate and the balance of payments

A further way in which an increase in interest rates leads to a decrease in aggregate demand works through the effect of higher interest rates on net export demand $(X - M)$. A higher interest rate attracts capital flows into the UK. This causes the pound's exchange rate to rise, which makes UK exports less price competitive on world markets and imports more competitive in UK markets. The balance of payments on current account worsens, shifting the AD curve to the left. A cut in interest rates has the opposite effect.

Knowledge check 16

How might an increase in interest rates affect the consumption decisions of households with large mortgages?

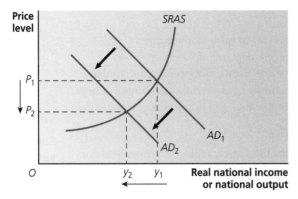

Figure 17 Raising interest rates decreases aggregate demand in contractionary monetary policy

Fiscal policy

Fiscal policy is the part of a government's economic policy aimed at achieving its economic objectives through the use of the fiscal instruments of taxation, public spending and the budget deficit or surplus. Until quite recently, fiscal policy was implemented solely by the chancellor of the exchequer, who is in charge of the Treasury.

This has now partially changed. Before 2010, many politicians and economists argued that fiscal policy should be made operationally independent of the Treasury, in much the same way that the implementation of monetary policy had been separated from government by being passed over to the Bank of England back in 1997.

Although this has not happened (the Treasury remains firmly in control of fiscal policy), in 2010 George Osborne, the incoming Conservative chancellor of the Coalition government, created the **Office for Budget Responsibility (OBR)** to provide independent analysis of the UK's public sector finances. The OBR produces forecasts for the economy and public finances.

The Treasury still produces the bulk of the forecasting but the OBR rather than the chancellor is in charge of the Treasury's forecasting team. And instead of the chancellor making judgements based on Treasury forecasts, the OBR rules on whether the government's policy has a better than 50% chance of meeting the fiscal targets set by the Treasury.

Demand-side fiscal policy

For many years, fiscal policy was generally associated with managing the level of aggregate demand in order to expand (reflate) or contract (deflate) the economy. This became known as Keynesian fiscal policy or **demand-side fiscal policy**. To increase aggregate demand, the government increased government spending or cut taxes. The resulting increase in the government's budget deficit injected demand into the circular flow of income. This was expansionary fiscal policy. By contrast, contractionary fiscal policy involved the opposite: cuts in government spending or tax increases that reduced the budget deficit, possibly moving the government's finances into surplus. Contractionary (or deflationary) fiscal policy took demand out of the economy.

Office for Budget Responsibility (OBR) A government agency which provides the Treasury with independent analysis of the UK's public sector finances. The OBR produces forecasts for the economy and public finances.

Demand-side fiscal policy Fiscal policy that aims to change the level of aggregate demand in the economy.

Exam tip

Whereas fiscal policy can affect aggregate demand by changing the level of government spending (G), monetary policy affects the other components of aggregate demand, C, I and (X – M).

Content Guidance

Discretionary fiscal policy

When fiscal policy has been used in a Keynesian way to raise or lower taxes and government spending so as to manage aggregate demand, it has been called **discretionary fiscal policy**. This type of fiscal policy involves fine-tuning (or regularly adjusting) tax rates and levels of government spending in an attempt to maintain a high level of employment, while avoiding an unacceptable increase in the rate of inflation.

Free-market or supply-side fiscal policy

During recent decades, **supply-side fiscal policy** has largely replaced demand-side or Keynesian fiscal policy. Supply-side fiscal policy is part of a wider supply-side policy that aims to shift the *LRAS* curve to the right. In supply-side fiscal policy, taxes are cut, not to increase aggregate demand, but to increase incentives to work harder, to be entrepreneurial, to take risks and to invest. Under monetarist and supply-side influence, recent UK governments, with the exception of the short period of fiscal stimulus between 2008 and 2010, have generally believed that using fiscal policy in a demand-side way to stimulate or reflate aggregate demand to achieve growth and full employment is, in the long run, at best ineffective and at worst damaging. They have argued that any growth of output and employment resulting from an expansionary fiscal policy is short-lived, and that the main effect of such a policy is inflation, which quickly destroys the conditions necessary for satisfactory market performance and wealth creation. Supply-side policies and fiscal policy have also been used to create stability in the economy, so that economic agents, particularly businesses, are not subjected to sudden surprises in the form of unexpected tax changes.

Fiscal stimulus and fiscal austerity

However, for the short period just noted from 2008 to 2010, in response to deep recession, there was a complete U-turn in UK fiscal policy, which once again became Keynesian. Taxes were cut while government spending, the budget deficit and borrowing increased. But the Keynesian fiscal stimulus came to an end, partly due to a change of government and partly because the rapid increase in government borrowing appeared to be getting out of control. The Coalition government in power between 2010 and 2015, dominated by the Conservatives, favoured a return to supply-side fiscal policy. Government spending was cut, and fiscal austerity or fiscal consolidation replaced the fiscal stimulus.

The use of an automatic fiscal policy rule

By rejecting demand-side or Keynesian fiscal policy, supporters of supply-side fiscal policy also generally reject the use of discretionary fiscal policy. Many have also argued that the government should use an automatic fiscal policy rule always to balance the budget, i.e. to set *G* equal to *T*. Budget deficits and surpluses must not be allowed to occur. Indeed, in October 2015, the Conservative government enshrined into law a **fiscal charter** (the Charter for Budget Responsibility) that compels the government to achieve a surplus on its budget by 2019/20, and then in 'normal' years to keep the budget in surplus each year thereafter.

The microeconomic elements of fiscal policy

Unlike monetary policy, fiscal policy is used in a microeconomic as well as in a macroeconomic way. As already noted, supply-side fiscal policy focuses on the incentives and disincentives that result respectively from low and high tax rates.

Discretionary fiscal policy Fiscal policy in which the government 'fine-tunes' aggregate demand to try to stabilise the economic cycle.

Supply-side fiscal policy Fiscal policy which aims to create incentives in order to improve the economy's supply-side performance.

Exam tip

Exam questions may require you to have knowledge and understanding of recent events in the UK economy.

Fiscal charter The current fiscal charter was enshrined by the Conservative government into UK law late in 2015. The charter commits UK governments to achieving budget surpluses in the public finances. It replaced a fiscal charter introduced by the government before the May 2015 general election.

On the government-spending side of microeconomic fiscal policy, changes to the benefits system (particularly cuts in unemployment benefits and tax credits paid to low-paid workers) are made to alter the labour or leisure choice in favour of working rather than choosing voluntary unemployment. The Conservative government argues that these changes favour 'strivers' and punish 'shirkers'. The government's opponents, by contrast, claim that the main effect is to increase poverty among both the unemployed and low-paid workers.

At the macro level, fiscal policy affects the *level* of economic activity, while at the micro level, fiscal policy affects the *pattern* of economic activity, for example through state provision of public goods and merit goods, and through the use of expenditure taxes and subsidies to alter the relative prices of goods and services. (This element of fiscal policy, which is part of the microeconomic specifications at both AS and A-level, is assessed by exam questions on market failure in the Unit 1 exams.)

Using AD/AS diagrams to analyse demand-side fiscal policy

As we have noted, demand-side fiscal policy or Keynesian fiscal policy operates through increasing or decreasing aggregate demand. Government spending (G) is one of the components of aggregate demand. An increase in government spending or a cut in taxation increases the size of the budget deficit (or reduces the size of the budget surplus). Either way, an injection into the circular flow of income occurs and the effect on aggregate demand is expansionary.

Figure 18 illustrates the effect of such an expansionary or reflationary fiscal policy. Initially, with the aggregate demand curve in position AD_1, macroeconomic equilibrium occurs at point X. Real income or output is y_1, and the price level is P_1.

To eliminate the cyclical (demand-deficient or Keynesian) unemployment, the government increases the budget deficit by raising the level of government spending or by cutting taxes. The expansionary fiscal policy shifts the AD curve to the right from AD_1 to AD_2, and the economy moves to a new macroeconomic equilibrium at point Z.

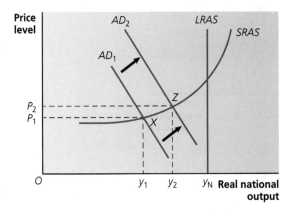

Figure 18 Keynesian or demand-side fiscal policy

As we explained earlier, the extent to which expansionary fiscal policy reflates real output (in this case from y_1 to y_2), or creates excess demand that leads to demand-pull inflation (in this case an increase in the price level from P_1 to P_2), depends on the shape of the AS curve, which in turn depends on how close initially the economy was to full employment, which we are assuming occurs when the economy is producing the 'normal' capacity level of output, y_N. The nearer the economy gets to full employment and 'normal' capacity, the greater the inflationary effect of expansionary fiscal policy and the smaller the reflationary effect.

Figure 18 can be adapted to illustrate the effect of a contractionary or deflationary fiscal policy. In this case a cut in government spending or an increase in taxation shifts the AD curve to the left.

Fiscal policy and the government spending multiplier

When fiscal policy is used in a macroeconomic way to manage aggregate demand, an important concept that helps to explain the relationship between a change in G and the resulting change in national income (Y) is the size of the **government spending multiplier**. For example, if the value of the multiplier is 2, an initial increase in government spending of £10 billion increases nominal national income by £20 billion. However, the increase in *nominal* output may in part be an increase in the price level rather than an increase in *real* output. Whether real output increases or the price level increases depends on the shape of the $SRAS$ curve, which in turn depends on how close the initial level of output was to the $LRAS$ curve and to 'normal' capacity.

Fiscal policy and possible crowding out

Many free-market or anti-Keynesian economists believe that, besides causing inflation rather than an increase in real output, another significant effect of an increase in government spending is to crowd out private sector spending. The production possibility frontier in Figure 19 shows how **crowding out** takes place.

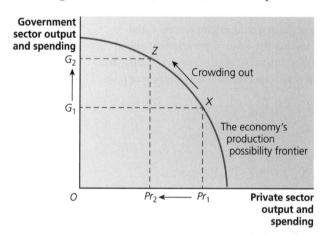

Figure 19 Government spending crowding out private sector spending

If the economy is initially at point X on its production possibility frontier, an increase in government spending from G_1 to G_2 displaces or crowds out private spending by Pr_1 minus Pr_2. The new combination of government spending and private sector spending is shown at point Z on the production possibility frontier. Government spending grows at the expense of private sector spending, but because the economy is assumed to be on its production possibility frontier, there is no overall increase in

---

Knowledge check 17

Contrast the government spending and the investment multiplier. Name two other multipliers.

Government spending multiplier Measures the relationship between a change in government spending and the resulting change in the equilibrium level of nominal national income.

Crowding out A situation in which an increase in government or public sector spending displaces private sector spending, with little or no increase in aggregate demand.

output. The opposite of crowding out is 'crowding in'. According to Chancellor George Osborne this occurs when public spending cuts free up resources for the private sector to use.

How taxation affects the economy

Taxation is used to finance government spending, though when there is a budget deficit government borrowing also finances public spending. As already noted, expenditure taxes and subsidies alter economic behaviour by changing the relative prices of goods and services. Taxation also reduces the amount of income that people have available to spend on consumption or imports.

The effect of progressive taxation

Progressive taxation leads to the rich paying a larger proportion of their income on taxes than the poor. Keynesian governments transferred the revenue raised from progressive taxation to the poor, in the form of welfare benefits. This altered the distribution of income in favour of lower-income groups. As a result, patterns of production and spending changed away from goods and services consumed by the better-off to those consumed by the poor. However, in recent years the progressivity of the UK tax and benefits systems has generally been reduced, with the result that income inequalities have usually widened.

Progressive taxation and incentives

Free-market economists believe that progressive taxation and transfers to the poor have a bad effect on personal incentives, reducing the incentives to work and to be entrepreneurial, while increasing the incentive to live off benefits. The supply-side fiscal policy advocated by free-market economists attempts to reduce taxation, government spending and the size of the state, thereby freeing up resources for the private sector to use.

Supply-side policies

Before the 1980s, macroeconomic policy generally meant demand management. However, in the 1980s and 1990s, economic policy switched away from the demand side to the supply side of the economy. Economists now generally agree that, except in recessions, the major problems facing the UK economy are the supply-side problems of producing goods and services that are both quality competitive and price competitive in domestic and export markets.

Supply-side policies, which in part are a response to increasingly fierce international competition, aim to change the underlying structure of the economy. Tax changes designed to change personal incentives try to increase potential output and improve the underlying trend rate of economic growth. Supply-side policies also affect the level of unemployment, the inflation rate and UK external performance as reflected in the balance of payments.

Many supply-side policies are microeconomic rather than macroeconomic, since they act on the motivation and efficiency of individual economic agents to improve economic performance. If successful, such policies also have a macroeconomic effect by shifting the economy's long-run aggregate supply curve to the right.

Knowledge check 18

What is the meant by supply-side 'crowding in'?

....

Progressive taxation
A tax system in which the rich pay a larger proportion of their income in tax than the poor.

Knowledge check 19

What is the difference between progressive and regressive taxation?

....

Supply-side fiscal policy

As we have mentioned, since the 1980s supply-side fiscal policy has largely replaced demand-side fiscal policy. (We noted that monetary policy rather than fiscal policy has been used to manage aggregate demand.) Between 1979 and the early 2000s, successive UK governments cut income tax rates on several occasions. However, governments did this, not for Keynesian reasons to stimulate aggregate demand, but to create supply-side incentives in the economy. As we have also explained, supply-side economists believe that income tax cuts create incentives to work harder, to be entrepreneurial and to take financial risks, to save and to invest in new capital equipment.

Other parts of supply-side fiscal policy have been:

- reducing state welfare benefits to create an incentive to choose low-paid employment rather than unemployment
- granting special tax privileges for savings
- reducing public spending, budget deficits and government borrowing to free up resources for private sector use. Supply-side economists believe that the public sector is too big and that it 'crowds out' the private sector. Cutting the size of the public sector and its need to borrow will, by providing room for it to grow, 'crowd in' the private sector.

Other supply-side policies

Supply-side policies, other than supply-side fiscal policy, can be grouped into three main categories.

Industrial policy measures

These include:

- **privatisation** — the sale or transfer of assets such as nationalised industries from the public sector to the private sector
- **marketisation** — the shifting of economic activity from non-market provision financed by taxation to market provision
- **deregulation** — the removal of previously imposed regulations in order to promote competition by removing barriers to market entry and to get rid of unnecessary red tape and bureaucracy, which raise firms' costs

Labour market measures

These include:

- increasing labour market flexibility — by reducing the powers of trade unions and replacing jobs for life with short-term labour contracts
- improving the training of labour

Financial market and capital market measures

These include:

- deregulating financial markets — to create greater competition and lower borrowing costs (though since the financial crisis of 2007–8 there has been a certain amount of re-regulation)
- encouraging saving by selling government-owned shares in privatised industries — to encourage wider share ownership

---

Exam tip

Remember that fiscal policy can be used in a supply-side way as well as for managing the level of aggregate demand in the economy.

Knowledge check 20

Why do supply-side economists support income tax cuts?

Privatisation The transfer of firms or industries from the public sector to the private sector, usually when the government sells firms or industries to private individuals or financial institutions.

Marketisation The transfer of economic activity from the non-market sector of the economy, where goods and services are often provided free to consumers, to the market sector, where goods and services are sold at market prices.

Deregulation The removal of previously imposed regulations.

Using AD/AS diagrams to analyse supply-side policies

Supply-side policies aim to shift the economy's long-run aggregate supply curve (*LRAS*) curve to the right, thereby increasing the economy's potential level of output. The effect of successful supply-side fiscal policy on the *LRAS* curve is shown in Figure 20. (Note that an outward movement of the economy's production possibility frontier can also illustrate the intended effect of supply-side policies.)

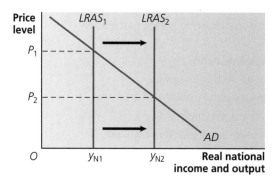

Figure 20 Supply-side policies shifting the *LRAS* curve to the right

Figure 20 illustrates another possible result of successful supply-side policy, namely a 'good deflation'. Supply-side policies can lead to an outcome in which invention and innovation reduce business costs (and thence the price level) at the same time as promoting economic growth and higher levels of output and employment. In Figure 20, the increase in long-run aggregate supply causes real output to rise from y_{N1} to y_{N2}, and the price level to fall from P_1 to P_2.

Knowledge check 21

Why is productivity important for supply-side economists?

The impact of supply-side policy on the national economy

From 1992 until 2008, the UK economy benefited from continuous economic growth. Many economists argued that, by making markets more efficient and competitive, supply-side policies were vital in promoting and elongating the boom years. Such economists subscribed to the dictum 'first the pain and then the gain'. The pain was high unemployment and widening income inequalities, which were blamed on supply-side policies in their early years. The gain was the continuous economic growth that then kicked in, once the appropriate supply-side conditions were in place.

However, other conditions may also have improved national economic performance. These included the success of monetary policy in managing demand, and perhaps 'luck' in the form of benign conditions in an increasingly globalised world economy. Whichever view is correct, supply-side policies have widened income inequalities, although most of the growing inequality may result more from the adverse effects of globalisation than from supply-side policies per se.

The private sector's role in improving the supply side of the economy

Supply-side policy is almost always pro-market and anti-interventionist. It attempts to change the function of government from *provider* to *enabler*. Supply-side policies aim to promote entrepreneurship and popular capitalism, replacing the dependency culture and statism, which — for the supply-siders — are the legacy of previous demand-side economic policy. But supply-side policy cannot deliver unless the private sector does its job in improving labour productivity, innovation and investment.

Supply-side reforms undertaken by firms, such as the reorganisation of methods of production, are arguably as important as government policy in bringing about required change in the structure of the economy.

Supply-side reforms
Reforms undertaken by private-sector firms to make themselves more efficient and competitive.

Examination skills

The skills most likely to be tested by multiple-choice or data-response questions on macroeconomic policy are as follows:

- Relating monetary policy to the objectives of macroeconomic policy, particularly the control of inflation.
- Explaining how monetary policy affects aggregate demand.
- Illustrating the effects of monetary policy with an *AD/AS* diagram.
- Defining fiscal policy and distinguishing it from monetary policy.
- Understanding links between fiscal policy and monetary policy.
- Explaining how fiscal policy can be used to manage aggregate demand and discussing the limitations of using fiscal policy in this way.
- Illustrating demand-side fiscal policy on an *AD/AS* diagram and explaining how the effectiveness of the policy depends on the nature of aggregate supply.
- Describing and explaining the main elements of supply-side fiscal policy implemented in the UK in recent years.
- Applying in a relevant way fiscal policy concepts such as the budget deficit or surplus, and government or public-sector borrowing that finances a deficit.
- Identifying a range of supply-side policies.
- Relating supply-side policy to free-market views of how the economy works and the appropriate approach of economic policy to problems posed by the economy.
- Illustrating the impact of supply-side policies on an *AD/AS* diagram.
- Comparing and contrasting the effects of supply-side and demand-side policies.
- Evaluating the effectiveness of supply-side policy, perhaps with the aid of appropriate indicators of national economic performance, such as productivity figures.

Examination questions

In AS Paper 2, you should expect up to four of the 20 multiple-choice questions to be set on macroeconomic policy, with possibly one question asking for a calculation. In A-level Paper 3, you should expect up to two of the 30 multiple-choice questions (which cover both microeconomics and macroeconomics) to be on macroeconomic policy, with a calculation possibly involved. See MCQs 10, 11 and 12 on pages 59–60 for examples, though neither of these questions requires a calculation. DRQs 3 (page 76) and 6 (page 100) focus, respectively, on fiscal policy and monetary policy.

Common examination errors

Commonly made mistakes on macroeconomic policy are:

- confusing fiscal policy with monetary policy
- inability to use an *AD/AS* diagram to illustrate the impact of fiscal policy on the national economy
- confusing a budget deficit (or surplus) with a balance of payments deficit (or surplus)

- inability to relate a budget deficit (or surplus) to injections into (or withdrawals from) the circular flow of income
- failure to understand that many aspects of recent and current fiscal policy in the UK illustrate supply-side economic policy
- poor understanding of concepts such as progressive taxation and transfers

Summary

- Monetary policy is the part of a government's economic policy aimed at achieving the government's economic objectives through the use of the monetary instruments.
- In the UK, monetary policy is implemented by the country's central bank, the Bank of England, but aims to hit an inflation rate target set by the government.
- The Bank of England's interest rate, called Bank Rate, is the main monetary policy instrument in the UK. Bank Rate is set each month by the Monetary Policy Committee of the Bank of England.
- From 2009 until 2012, quantitative easing (QE) was used to supplement interest policy.
- Knowledge of QE is required at A-level but not at AS.
- Monetary policy is used to manage aggregate demand in a way consistent with achieving the monetary policy target set by the government.
- Raising or lowering interest rates affects C, I and $(X - M)$ and hence the position of the AD curve.
- From 2008 until at least 2015 monetary policy has been used to help the UK recover from recession, and during this period the inflation rate target was somewhat ignored.

- Fiscal policy is the part of a government's economic policy aimed at achieving its economic objectives through the use of the fiscal instruments.
- Fiscal policy instruments are taxation, public spending and the budget deficit or surplus.
- Demand-side fiscal policy, or Keynesian fiscal policy, manages aggregate demand.
- Along with other supply-side policies, supply-side fiscal policy aims to shift the $LRAS$ curve to the right.
- Supply-side fiscal policy tries to create incentives by cutting tax rates and making it less attractive to claim welfare benefits.
- Supply-side fiscal policy is often microeconomic rather than macroeconomic.
- Taxation is used to finance government spending, as is government borrowing.
- Progressive taxation and transfers of tax revenue to lower income groups reduce income inequality, but may also adversely affect incentives.

Questions & Answers

AS Paper 2 and A-level Paper 2

At AS, Paper 2, 'The national economy in a global context', is 1 hour 30 minutes long and has a maximum mark of 70. The exam paper contains two sections, A and B, both of which must be answered. Section A, which accounts for 20 marks (about 29% of the total), comprises 20 compulsory multiple-choice questions (MCQs). One mark will be awarded for each MCQ answered correctly. Section B accounts for 50 marks (just under 71% of the total) and comprises two data-response questions (DRQs), labelled Context 1 and Context 2, of which you should answer one.

At A-level, Paper 2, 'The national and international economy', is 2 hours long and has a maximum mark of 80. The exam paper contains two sections, A and B, both of which must be answered. Section A, which accounts for 40 marks (50% of the total), comprises two data-response questions (DRQs), labelled Context 1 and Context 2, of which you should answer one. Section B, which also accounts for 40 marks (50% of the total), contains three essay questions (EQs), of which you should answer one.

Note: No essay questions and answers are included in this guide. Essays account for 50% of total assessment in the A-level Paper 1 and Paper 2 exams, but they are not a part of AS assessment. You will find sample essay questions, with student answers at Grades A or A* and at Grade C, in *Student Guides* 3 and 4.

A-level Paper 3

Besides including a case study investigation (coverage of which is included in *Student Guides* 3 and 4 rather than in this guide), the A-level Paper 3 exam has 30 MCQs, of which roughly half are on microeconomics and roughly half on macroeconomics. The MCQs that follow in this guide are similar to those in both the AS Paper 2 exam and the A-level Paper 3 exam.

Assessment objectives

Assessment objectives (AOs) are set by a government agency, Ofqual, and are the same across the AS and A-level economics specifications. The exams measure how students have achieved the following assessment objectives:

- AO1: Demonstrate knowledge of terms/concepts and theories/models to show an understanding of the behaviour of economic agents (consumers, workers and firms) and how they are affected by and respond to economic issues.
  Weighting: AS 29–31%; A-level 20–23%.
- AO2: Apply knowledge and understanding to various economic contexts to show how economic agents are affected by and respond to economic issues.
  Weighting: AS 31–33%; A-level 26–29%.
- AO3: Analyse issues within economics, showing an understanding of their impact on economic agents. Weighting: AS 21–23%; A-level 26–29%.

■ AO4: Evaluate economic arguments and use qualitative and quantitative evidence to support informed judgements relating to economic issues. Weighting: AS 15–17%; A-level 22–25%.

AO1 and AO2 are testing 'lower-order' skills, whereas AO3 and AO4 test 'higher-order' skills. The testing of AO3 and AO4 is slightly more important at A-level than it is at AS.

The questions in this guide

This guide includes 18 examination-style questions designed to be a key learning, revision and exam preparation resource. For all students, there are 12 multiple-choice questions (MCQs). These are followed by six data-response questions (DRQs). Three of these (DRQ 1, 3 and 5) are AS questions. The other three (DRQ 2, 4 and 6) are A-level questions. All the DRQs contain three data extracts. AS students could use the A-level questions for revision purposes; likewise the AS questions might provide useful revision for A-level students.

All the questions in this guide can be used 'en bloc' as part of a short trial or mock exam near the end of your course. Alternatively, as you study a topic in the Content Guidance section of this guide, you could refer selectively to particular questions in this section that assess aspects of the topic.

This section of the guide also contains:

■ correct answers for the MCQs and comments on each question
■ comments on the DRQs, denoted by the icon ⓔ
■ student answers of A-grade standard (or sometimes A* standard for the A-level questions) and C-grade standard for each DRQ
■ comments on each student's answer explaining, where relevant, how the answer could be improved. These comments are denoted by the icon ⓔ.

■ Multiple-choice questions (MCQs)

Question 1 National income, economic growth and the economic cycle

Money national income for a country in 2016 is equal to:

A The physical quantity of goods and services produced in the country in 2016.

B Real national income in 2016 adjusted for inflation.

C The money value of the stock of capital and consumer goods in the country at the end of 2016.

D Real national income produced by the country's economy in 2016 valued at 2016's prices.

Question 2 Unemployment and inflation

The table below shows information about unemployment as a percentage of the labour force and the rate of inflation in an economy over a period.

Year	Unemployment (%)	Inflation (%)
2013	7.2	2.4
2014	7.0	2.1
2015	6.9	1.6
2016	6.8	1.4

From the data it can be concluded that over the period:

A Prices have fallen.

B Unemployment has fallen.

C Disinflation has taken place.

D A conflict exists between achieving falling rates of unemployment and inflation.

Question 3 Interpreting index numbers

The following table shows the figures for population, and the index numbers for the CPI and nominal GDP in a particular economy for 2015 and 2016.

Year	Population (millions)	Consumer prices index	Nominal GDP
2015	40	100	100
2016	50	101	105

From the table it can be concluded that:

A Real GDP increased by 5% over the 2-year period.

B 2015 must have been the base year for both the consumer prices index and the nominal GDP index.

C Nominal GDP per capita decreased over the 2-year period.

D Real GDP per capita increased over the 2-year period.

Question 4 The circular flow of income

The diagram below shows the circular flow of income in an economy.

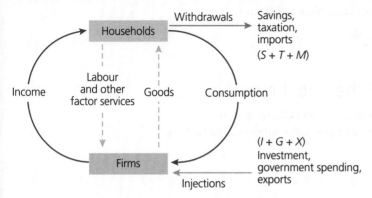

In the diagram, macroeconomic equilibrium occurs when:

A $S + T + M = I + G + X$.

B   Expenditure exceeds income and output.

C   All income is spent on consumption.

D   All goods are exchanged for money.

Question 5 The multiplier and the accelerator

An increase in investment of £1 billion causes national income to increase by £3 billion. The increase in national income then causes investment to increase by £2 billion. This information illustrates the:

A   Multiplier followed by the accelerator.

B   Multiplier only.

C   Accelerator followed by the multiplier.

D   Accelerator only.

Question 6 The *AD/AS* macroeconomic model

The diagram below shows a shift to the right of an economy's *AD* curve along its *LRAS* curve.

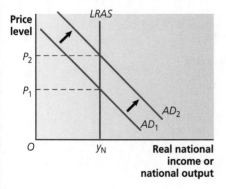

The diagram illustrates:

A   Cost-push inflation.

B   The movement to a new position of macroeconomic equilibrium.

C   The effect of successful supply-side policy.

D   The elimination of cyclical unemployment.

Question 7 The long run and the short run

The diagram below shows the aggregate demand curves (AD), long-run aggregate supply curve ($LRAS$) and the short-run aggregate supply curve ($SRAS$) for an economy.

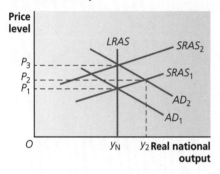

Compared to the situation in the initial equilibrium at y_N and P_1, the shift of the AD curve from AD_1 to AD_2 will:

A   Increase both output and the price level in the long run.

B   Leave the price level and real output unchanged in the long run.

C   Increase output but not the price level in the short run.

D   Increase the price level but not output in the long run.

Question 8 Policy instruments and policy objectives

Which of the following matched pairs of policy instruments and policy objectives makes most economic sense?

	Policy instrument	Policy objective
A	Income tax increase	Faster economic growth
B	Increased government spending	Improved balance of payments
C	Interest rate cut	More consumption and investment
D	Interest rate increase	Improved balance of payments

Question 9 Expansion and contraction of the economy

Which **one** of the following, if **decreased**, would be most likely to have an expansionary effect on an economy?

A   Imports of goods and services.

B   Public spending on infrastructure projects.

C   Exports of goods and services.

D   The rate of growth of the money supply.

Question 10 Monetary policy

When the economy is in recession, which of the following is **least** likely to reduce unemployment?

A   An expansionary monetary policy.

B   The Bank of England cutting interest rates.

C   Retraining schemes for redundant workers.

D   A new regulation extending employment rights for newly hired workers.

Question 11 Fiscal policy

Which of the following is an example of fiscal policy?

A   The Bank of England imposing controls on bank lending.

B   The removal of foreign exchange controls which restrict the transfer of currencies between countries.

C   The removal of regulations which restrict Sunday trading.

D   The creation of tax-exempt Individual Savings Accounts (ISAs).

Question 12 Supply-side policies

Which of the following statements about supply-side economics is correct?

A   Supply-side policies are used to improve the economy's efficiency and competitiveness.

B   Fiscal policy cannot be used as a part of supply-side policy.

C   Supply-side economists support the use of demand-management policies in all circumstances.

D   The main aim of supply-side policies is to increase aggregate demand.

Answers to multiple-choice questions

Question 1

Statement **A** provides a definition of *real* national income. However, the question asks for a definition of *money* national income. Money national income (or *nominal* national income) is real national income valued at current prices. Statement **B** is simply nonsense, while Statement **C** invites you to confuse flows with stocks. Statement **D** provides a correct definition and is the correct answer.

Question 2

Statement **C** provides the correct answer: disinflation is a slowing down in the rate of positive inflation, and this is shown by the data in the right-hand column of the table. The rate of inflation has fallen, but not the price level, so Statement **A** is incorrect. Statement **B** is incorrect: the table shows that the *percentage rate* of unemployment is falling. However, the unemployment *level* could still increase if the country's population was growing rapidly. Finally, because the percentage rates of both unemployment and inflation fell over the whole period, there was no conflict between 2013 and 2016 in achieving the two policy objectives. Statement **D** is thus wrong.

Question 3

Although nominal GDP increased by 5% (105 being 5% higher than 100), because the inflation rate was 1%, real GDP must have increased by less than this. This means that Statement **A** is incorrect. With regard to the second statement, 2015 *could* have been the base year for both the CPI and the nominal GDP index, but it *may not* have been. For a year other than the base year, an index number can by chance equal 100. Statement **B** therefore cannot be concluded from the data. Statement **C** does, however, provide the answer. As already stated, nominal GDP increased by 5% between the 2 years. However, population increased by more than 5% (10 million divided by 40 million, which is 25%). Lastly, real GDP as well as nominal GDP decreased between the 2 years, so Statement **D** is incorrect.

Question 4

Besides occurring at the level of real output at which *AD = AS*, macroeconomic equilibrium also occurs when leakages from the circular flow of income exactly equal injections into the flow. Statement A provides the latter definition and so is the correct answer. Statements B, C and D do not define macroeconomic equilibrium.

Question 5

The stem of the question indicates that two processes are operating, so Statements **B** and **D**, each of which is about only one process, must be wrong. This means that either Statement **A** or Statement **C** is correct. The multiplier shows the effect of an increase in a component of aggregate demand (in this case investment) on national income. The accelerator shows the reverse effect, namely how a change in national income affects investment. The stem indicates that the multiplier occurs first and is followed by the accelerator. This means that Statement **A** is correct and Statement **C** is the wrong way round.

Question 6

The correct answer is Statement **B**, as the economy moves to a new macroeconomic equilibrium at a higher price level, albeit at the same level of real national output. Cost-push inflation would be depicted by a leftward shift of the *SRAS* curve and a fall in real output. This is not shown on the diagram, so Statement **A** is wrong. Statements **C** and **D** are also wrong because successful supply-side policies would shift the *LRAS* curve to the right, while the elimination of cyclical unemployment would require the initial level of output to be below y_N.

Question 7

The distance from y_N to y_2 shows output *temporarily* increasing above the normal capacity level of output (y_N), but in the long run output falls back to y_N. In the long run, however, an upward shift of the *SRAS* curve from $SRAS_1$ to $SRAS_2$, caused by the increase in money wages needed to persuade workers to supply sufficient labour to produce output y_2, leads to the price level rising to P_3. The price level rises, however, to P_3. This means that Statement **A** is wrong and Statement **D** is correct: only the price level but not real output increases in the long run. Statements **B** and **C** are also wrong because they don't contain the correct pair of outcomes.

Question 8

Statement **C** is the correct answer: lower interest rates reduce the cost of borrowing and increase the incentive to save, thus stimulating consumption spending by households and investment spending on capital goods by firms. The other three policy changes would produce the opposite results to those stated in the policy objectives.

Question 9

When answering this question, you could use the equation $S + T + M = I + G + X$. The three variables on the left-hand side of the equality sign (=) are the three leakages or withdrawals of demand from the circular flow of income, while those on the right-hand side are injections into the circular flow. Statements **B**, **C** and **D** focus on injections into the circular flow of income. A *decrease* in any of these has a *contractionary* effect on the economy, so these do not provide the correct answer. This leaves Statement **A** as the appropriate answer: although imports (M) are a leakage of demand from the circular flow of income, a *decrease* in imports has an *expansionary* effect on the economy.

Question 10

Statements **A** and **B** would reduce unemployment in a recession by expanding aggregate demand. Retraining schemes for redundant workers (Statement **C**) might also be expected to reduce unemployment. This leaves Statement **D** as the correct answer: an extension of employment rights would make it more costly and less attractive for employers to hire workers. (Note the word 'least' in the stem of the question. If you fail to take account of this word, your answer is almost certain to be wrong.)

Question 11

Statements **A** and **B** are examples of monetary policy rather than fiscal policy, while Statement **C** provides an example of deregulation or the removal of direct controls on the economy. Statement **D** is an example of fiscal policy and therefore is the correct answer. ISAs encourage households to save rather than spend on consumption because interest paid on the savings is tax exempt.

Question 12

Statement **A** is the correct answer, providing a neat statement of the purpose of supply-side policy. Supply-side economists generally oppose the use of Keynesian policy, so Statement **C** is wrong. Statement **B** is also wrong: supply-side policies do involve fiscal policy, although to create incentives rather than to manage demand. Statement **D** is wrong because increasing aggregate demand is certainly not the direct aim of supply-side policy.

■ Data-response questions

Note: The various parts of the AS data-response questions that follow are numbered: [21], [22], [23], [24], [25] and [26]. This is because the DRQs follow the 20 MCQs in AS Paper 2. As there are no MCQs in A-level Paper 2, the various parts of the A-level DRQs that follow are numbered: [01], [02], [03] and [04] (Context 1) and [05], [06], [07] and [08] (Context 2).

Question 1 Productivity and investment (AS)

Context 1

Total for this Context: 50 marks

Study Extracts A, B and C, and then answer all parts of Context 1 which follow.

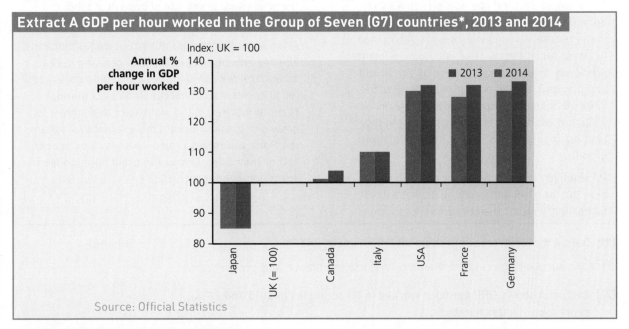

Extract A GDP per hour worked in the Group of Seven (G7) countries*, 2013 and 2014

Source: Official Statistics

Extract B The productivity puzzle

Officials at the Bank of England have been left scratching their heads by statistics that show the UK economy to be significantly less productive than they had expected, and less productive than many of its international rivals. 5

Since the onset of the 2007/08 financial crisis, labour productivity in the United Kingdom has been exceptionally weak. Despite some modest improvements in 2013, UK labour productivity remains, in 2014, around 16% below the level 10 implied by its pre-crisis trend.

Bank of England experts are puzzled by the UK's low labour productivity, but they have offered a series of possible explanations. These include the possibility that firms held on to workers whom 15 they didn't actually need during the recession, and a drop in investment over the same period.

With regard to the first possible explanation, companies may have retained staff, despite weak demand for their products, in the expectation that 20 they would be able to avoid the costs of firing and subsequent re-hiring when recovery occurred. This would be helped by the likelihood that increases in wage rates would remain subdued. And with regard to the fall in investment, 25 depressed business confidence could have led to the cancellation or postponement of planned investment decisions.

→

The Bank said, however, that these two factors are not enough to fully explain the productivity puzzle. 30 Other factors could be a drying up in the supply of funds to finance investment by progressive businesses in new technology, while at the same time banks being prepared to lend to so-called 'zombie' firms that should have been allowed 35 to go bust.

Earlier in 2014, the International Monetary Fund (IMF) cited low UK productivity as one of the key risks to Britain's economic outlook, alongside the threat from an overheating housing market. 40 The IMF said the durability of the recovery from 2014 onwards hinged on productivity growth, but warned this remained 'well below historic norms'.

Source: News reports, 2014

Extract C Solving the productivity puzzle

The Bank of England has now struck a more optimistic note on productivity growth, saying that in the recovery, rising wages will push companies to invest more and that this will boost economic efficiency. While banks propped up inefficient 5 companies in the years immediately after the 2007/08 financial crisis, there are signs in 2015 that capital has resumed flowing to the best businesses. This should boost economic growth. 10

Productivity is the main driver of living standards over the long run and economists warn it will be harder to repair the public finances unless there is a sustained rate of growth of labour productivity. 15

After several years of falling real wages since the 2008 recession, wages are now growing in real terms. But Sir Jon Cunliffe, the deputy governor for financial stability at the Bank of England, recently warned that if wages are to continue to 20 grow while labour productivity remains stagnant, the Bank will have to raise interest rates sooner rather than later, in order to avoid inflation from spiralling out of control.

Source: News reports, 2015

[21] Define the term 'labour productivity' (Extract B, line 7). [3 marks]

ⓔ Make sure you address both the words in the term, 'labour' and 'productivity'.

[22] Extract A shows GDP per hour worked in G7 countries in 2013 and 2014, expressed in index numbers.

Calculate, to one decimal place, GDP per hour worked in Italy in 2013 as a percentage of GDP per hour worked in Germany in 2013. [4 marks]

ⓔ Although the data are presented in index numbers, for this question all you are required to do is to perform a simple percentage calculation.

[23] Using Extract A, identify two significant points of comparison between the changes in GDP per hour worked in the seven countries shown in the data. [4 marks]

ⓔ A significant point of comparison could be between two of the countries shown in Extract A (provided it is indeed significant), or it could be in terms of more than two countries — perhaps all seven. However, the answer must focus on *changes* in GDP per hour worked.

[24] Lines 25–28 of Extract B state that 'with regard to the fall in investment, depressed business confidence could have led to the cancellation or postponement of planned investment decisions.' Draw an aggregate demand and short-run aggregate supply curve diagram to show how a fall in investment might affect real national output and the price level. [4 marks]

ⓔ Make sure you depict an appropriate shift of the *AD* curve.

[25] **Lines 36–40 of Extract B state that in 2014, the IMF cited the threat from an overheating housing market as one of the key risks to Britain's economic outlook.**

Explain why an overheating housing market may be a key risk to Britain's economic outlook. [10 marks]

ⓔ In order to pick up all the available marks for this question, it is probably best to provide at least two points of explanation, and for each to set out a 'logical chain of reasoning'.

[26] **In lines 18–24 of Extract C, the deputy governor for financial stability at the Bank of England warned that 'if wages are to continue to grow while labour productivity remains stagnant, the Bank will have to raise interest rates sooner rather than later, in order to avoid inflation from spiralling out of control'.**

Evaluate the deputy governor's view. [25 marks]

ⓔ You don't have to agree or disagree with the deputy governor, but you should outline his reasoning, weigh up its strengths and weaknesses, and possibly outline other relevant factors that he has not stated.

Student A

[21] Productivity is output per unit of input in a particular time period. It can be measured for each of the factors of production. For example, labour productivity is output per worker in a particular time period.

ⓔ **3/3 marks awarded.** If the answer contained only the first sentence it would earn 2 but not 3 marks. The second sentence, which accurately defines labour productivity, on its own picks up all 3 marks.

[22] 110/130 x 100 = 84.615%

ⓔ **3/4 marks awarded.** The calculation is correct, but because the student has ignored the instruction to calculate to two decimal places, 1 mark has been lost. The correct answer is 84.62%, as 84.615% is rounded up to 84.62%.

[23] The first significant point of comparison is that Germany, France, the USA and Canada all saw labour productivity improvements compared with UK workers between 2013 and 2014. French labour productivity increased from 127 to 132 index points, German and American labour productivity increased from 130 to 133 and 132 index points respectively, and Canadian labour productivity increased from 101 to 105 index points.

The second significant point is that Japan is the only economy that suffered a GDP per hour work deterioration compared with the UK in both 2013 and 2014. In 2013 and 2014 the average Japanese worker produced 15% less GDP per hour than the average British worker.

ⓔ 4/4 marks awarded. A clear structure and two significant points of comparison are made and supported with evidence from the extract. For each comparison, 1 mark has been awarded for the comparison itself and 1 mark for the accurate statistical back-up. The comparisons are with the UK, but this is fine.

[24]

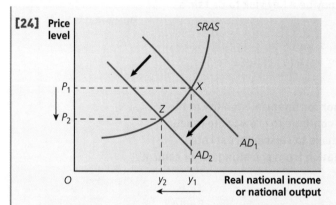

The fall in investment shifts the AD curve inwards from AD_1 to AD_2, causing real national output to fall from y_1 to y_2 and the price level to fall from P_1 to P_2.

ⓔ 4/4 marks awarded. The answer includes a correctly drawn diagram with accurate labelling and a brief explanation of the diagram.

[25] An overheated housing market could be a key risk to Britain's economic outlook because if the market crashes it will panic households and result in a consumer spending slowdown. This would happen in two ways.

First, a fall in house prices will make households feel poorer because the value of their main wealth assets will fall and they will cut back on expenditure. The 2011 Census reported that 63% of households in the UK were owner occupied. A house for most households is the most valuable asset that they own and it can take between 20 and 30 years to pay off the mortgage used to finance the house purchase. When house prices rise homeowners feel wealthier. When house prices fall they feel less well off. Therefore, a housing market crash will result in owner occupied households feeling poorer and cutting back on their consumption spending, which will reduce the most important component of aggregate demand and slow demand-side growth.

Second, a housing market crash is likely to result in financial instability. The majority of households take out a mortgage with a bank in order to buy their house. The mortgage is secured against the value of the property so if they default the bank can repossess the house. If the housing market crashes the banks will worry about lending and tighten up borrowing requirements. This will cut off sources of finance for both households and firms. Growth will then slow.

ⓔ 9/10 marks awarded. This answer is focused on the question and displays sound knowledge of economic terminology. The analysis is clear and the chain of reasoning is logical. The effects of falling house prices are analysed well.

However, one significant omission is an explanation of *why* an overheated housing market should lead to a fall in house prices. The answer reaches a high Level 3.

[26] The deputy governor is right to be concerned about the lack of labour productivity improvements in the UK economy because 'productivity is the main driver of living standards over the long run' (Extract C). If the economy is to grow in the long run firms need to invest in capital equipment and their workers' skills. By doing so firms become more productive and the output produced will increase. This will lead to economic growth and the economy's GDP increasing, which should translate into higher living standards.

The deputy governor's view is that if wages increase faster than the economy grows, inflationary pressures will enter the economy and the Monetary Policy Committee at the Bank of England will have to increase interest rates to prevent excess aggregate demand from creating inflation. This is a logical position for the governor to take but higher interest rates may not be the best policy for the Bank of England to pursue.

One of the main reasons for low labour productivity growth has been a lack of investment since the financial crisis in 2008. According to Extract B, firms did not invest because business confidence was depressed and led to 'the cancellation or postponement of planned investment decisions'. It makes no sense for the deputy governor to argue that interest rates should be increased if one of the problems is the lack of investment. An increase in interest rates will not encourage firms to borrow to invest. Higher interest rates will discourage investment because the cost of borrowing will increase. Instead the Bank of England should consider how it can help investment in 'progressive businesses in new technology' (Extract B). These firms could not get hold of finance during the recession and did not grow as quickly as they might otherwise have done.

A second reason why increasing interest rates is a bad idea is that it will reduce aggregate demand. If the MPC increases interest rates it will reduce consumption spending in the economy. This will help keep inflation down but it will also mean that firms will have reduced demand for their products. Given that one of the reasons for low labour productivity was that many firms 'held on to workers whom they didn't actually need during the recession' (Extract B), it seems that businesses could handle an increase in demand without putting up prices. Therefore, it is likely that the UK economy is operating below its capacity and there is a negative output gap, meaning that interest rates should be kept down and the economy will grow without inflation. If the UK economy is to grow without inflation and raise living standards then improvements in labour productivity are essential. However, the deputy governor is wrong to suggest that interest rates should be increased. Investment is the key to long-term growth and higher interest rates will discourage firms from borrowing money to invest. Instead the bank needs to look at ways of helping progressive companies and ensuring that they have the finance to produce world-class products.

ⓔ **20/25 marks awarded.** This is a high Level 4 answer. Level 4, which covers the range 16–20 marks, requires sound, focused analysis and some supported evaluation. The analysis is well focused and evidence is used from the extracts to support the points being made. The student makes judgements based on logical reasoning. The answer could explain how cost-push inflation might result from wages rising faster than labour productivity. Then diagrams could be used to illustrate demand-pull inflation and cost-push inflation. There is no concluding paragraph, so the answer lacks a strong final judgement.

ⓔ **Total score: 43/50 marks = Grade A**

Student B

[21] Labour productivity is how much output a typical worker can make.

ⓔ **2/3 marks awarded.** The answer is largely correct but needs to specify a particular period of time. 1 mark is deducted for this omission.

[22] The answer is 84.62%.

ⓔ **4/4 marks awarded.** The answer is correct although no workings are shown. It is always best to show workings, which may pick up some of the marks if a slip is made in the calculation.

[23] German workers were the most productive workers in the G7 in 2014 and Japanese workers were the least productive.

French workers' productivity increased the most between 2013 and 2014 when compared with UK workers.

ⓔ **1/4 marks awarded.** The first point earns no marks because it does not refer to *changes* in labour productivity and shows a misunderstanding of what index numbers indicate. The second point of comparison earns 1 of the available 2 marks. No marks at all have been awarded for statistical back-up, because there isn't any.

[24]

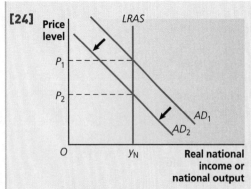

The fall in investment causes the AD curve to shift leftward from AD_1 to AD_2. The price level falls from P_1 to P_2, but real national output remains unchanged at y_N.

e **2/4 marks awarded.** Unfortunately the student has misread the question and drawn a vertical *LRAS* curve rather than an upward-sloping *SRAS* curve. However, 2 marks are awarded because the explanation is consistent with the diagram that has been drawn.

[25] If the housing market crashes it will be really bad for Britain. Housing is really important and loads of people want to buy a house, which they can do by borrowing money from a bank. If the housing market crashes, banks will stop lending money because they will not want to give money to buy houses that are crashing. This will make consumers feel bad because those that want to buy a house will not be given it from the bank while those that own a house will feel sad that their home is worth less. This will be really bad for the economy because everyone will stop spending and the retail sector will suffer. Shops will go bust or sack their workers because they are not selling enough. This will create a negative multiplier effect and *AD* will keep on shifting left.

e **5/10 marks awarded.** As is the case with the A-grade answer, the student does not explain why an overheated housing market should lead to a fall in house prices. However, several relevant points about the effects of falling house prices are made, though the analysis is weak and generally devoid of logical chains of reasoning. A mid-Level 2 mark is awarded.

[26] Inflation is the erosion of the value of money. The Bank of England sets interest rates in order to control the level of inflation. The MPC's inflation target is 2% measured by the CPI. There are two types of inflation: demand-pull and cost-push. Demand-pull is when there is an increase in the level of aggregate demand, which creates economic growth but also brings inflation into the economy. Cost-push is when the costs of production increase for firms and they have to increase their prices, which in turn leads to a fall in demand in the economy. If inflation increases then it makes sense that the deputy governor of the Bank of England will call for higher interest rates because inflation is rising.

If firms are paying workers more money, then workers will have more disposable income. This will mean that they can spend more money on consumption. Aggregate demand has five components and is calculated using the formula $AD = C + I + G + (X - M)$. Consumption is the most important component and accounts for approximately 65% of total planned aggregate demand in the economy. This will mean that if workers' incomes increase and consumption spending increases then there will be an increase in the level of aggregate demand in the economy. If excess demand is created it leads to demand-pull inflation, so the deputy governor is correct that interest rates will need to go up to control inflation.

The best way to keep inflation down is to implement supply-side policies. These are policies that enhance the capacity of the economy. If the government wants to improve the economy and create long-term economic

> growth it needs to pursue these policies. Good supply-side policies will improve productivity because workers will be better trained and have better skills. So rather than worrying about interest rates the government should focus on supply-side policies, which improve the capacity of the economy and create long-term economic growth.

ⓔ 12/25 marks awarded. The answer meets the Level 3 requirement of some reasonable analysis but there is generally unsupported evaluation. Within this level, it meets the requirements of focusing on issues that are relevant to the question, showing reasonable knowledge and understanding of economic terminology, concepts and principles. However, some analytical weaknesses are present and the evaluation is thin.

ⓔ Total score: 26/50 marks = Grade C

Question 2 Economic recovery from recession (A-level)

Context 1

Total for this Context: 40 marks

Study Extracts A, B and C, and then answer all parts of Context 1 which follow.

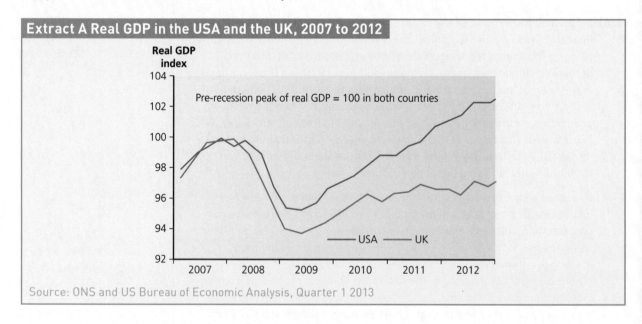

Extract A Real GDP in the USA and the UK, 2007 to 2012

Source: ONS and US Bureau of Economic Analysis, Quarter 1 2013

Extract B Why has US recovery been better than ours?

Why was the US recovery since the global crisis stronger than in the UK, particularly since mid-2010? The shocks were almost the same for both countries, but one of the key differences was in consumption behaviour. 5

Consumption grew more strongly in the USA than in the UK, with consumption growth stagnating in the UK from spring 2010 onward. (However, by 2015, UK consumption spending had picked up again.) 10

There were a number of reasons why consumption spending stagnated in 2010. These included:
■ Compared with the USA, growing unemployment raised uncertainty in the UK, and this depressed consumption. Fiscal policy differences also played an important role. Cumulatively, the UK government 15

tightened fiscal policy by 3% more than the US government did — taking local governments and automatic stabilisers into account — and this had a material impact on consumption. This was particularly the case because a large chunk of UK fiscal consolidation in 2010 and in 2011 took the form of a VAT increase, which has a high multiplier effect on household consumption. 20 25
■ The fact that British real incomes were hit harder than US household incomes by energy price increases, which were in part caused by the depreciation in 2008 of the pound's exchange rate, also hit real incomes directly. 30

All combined, these factors significantly dampened consumption growth in the UK, with knock-on effects on investment in new capital goods. 35

Source: News reports, 2015

Extract C UK recessions

The Office for National Statistics (ONS) regularly revises its published statistics. When this happens, the beginning, end and depth of recessions (and of periods of positive growth) can change. Before the ONS published revised statistics in 2013, the official view was that the UK economy in 2012 had entered the second dip of a 'double-dip' recession. Some economists were even predicting that a 'third dip' was on the cards. The revised statistics — if they can be trusted — show that the 'double dip' did not happen. The new statistics led to newspaper headlines such as the Daily Mail's: 'The recession that never was: the small change which makes a big difference'. 5 10

Updating its data in June 2013, the ONS said growth was flat in the first quarter of 2012, 15

revised from an earlier estimate of a 0.1% contraction. This means the economy did not contract for two quarters in a row — the definition of a recession. 20

But the ONS said the recession in 2008 was deeper than previously estimated. When the revised statistics were published, an ONS spokesperson commented 'We've had pretty gradual, fairly bumpy growth'. Lee Hopley, chief economist at the EEF manufacturers' organisation, said: 'Output across the economy and manufacturing has made up less ground since the end of the recession than previously thought and signs of any sustained rebalancing of the economy towards trade and investment remain elusive.' 25 30

Source: News reports, 2013

[01] Using the data in Extract A, calculate the percentage change in real GDP in the UK between the pre-recession peak early in 2008 and the end of Quarter 4 in 2012.

[2 marks]

ⓔ The wording of a Part [01] question at A-level involves the same sort of calculation as is involved in Part [02] of an AS question (see DRQ 1 on pages 61–63). However, only 2 marks are available at A-level, compared with 4 marks at AS.

[02] Making use of the data in Extracts A and B, explain ONE reason why, between 2009 and 2012, the UK's recovery from recession differed from the recovery in the US economy. [4 marks]

ⓔ The instruction to 'explain' is at the beginning of Parts [02] and [03] questions at A-level. Note that as a Part [02] question carries fewer marks (4 marks compared with 9 marks), the answer should be shorter than for the question that follows.

[03] Lines 6–8 of Extract B state: 'Consumption grew more strongly in the USA than in the UK, with consumption growth stagnating in the UK from spring 2010 onward'.

With the aid of an appropriate diagram, explain how a slowing down of consumption growth may affect UK macroeconomic performance. [9 marks]

ⓔ To reach the highest level in the mark scheme (7–9 marks) a diagram must be included in the answer to Part [03] questions at A-level. In this case, an *AD/AS* diagram is most appropriate, though other diagrams, such as a circular flow diagram, might also be appropriate. Make sure you briefly explain the meaning of 'UK macroeconomic performance'.

[04] Lines 27–31 of Extract C state: 'Output across the economy and manufacturing has made up less ground since the end of the recession than previously thought and signs of any sustained rebalancing of the economy towards trade and investment remain elusive.'

Do you agree that the UK economy must be rebalanced towards trade and investment for sustained economic growth to occur? Justify your answer. [25 marks]

ⓔ Part [04] questions require evaluation in the answers. When you are asked to agree or disagree with an assertion stated in the question, it is generally not wise to agree completely (or to disagree completely) with the assertion, but to argue, and then to justify your argument, that 'it all depends' on the assumptions you are making. One set of assumptions might lead to agreement, but alternative assumptions could lead to the opposite result. Make sure you define the two key concepts in the question: 'rebalancing the economy' and 'sustained economic growth'.

Student A

[01] UK real GDP decreased by approximately 3.3% between the economy's pre-recession peak in 2008 and the end of Quarter 4 in 2012.

ⓔ **2/2 marks awarded.** Note two points about the answer and the question. First, because the index number early in 2008 is 100, the percentage change that occurs between early 2008 and the end of Q4 2012 is the same as the index number change. This would not be the case if the starting-off index number were not 100. Second, because it is difficult to read accurately the index number at the end of 2012, the examiners would mark as correct any answer between about 3.1% and 3.4%.

[02] One reason why the UK recovered from the recession more slowly than the USA was because growing UK unemployment depressed consumption in a way that did not happen in the USA. Unemployment will reduce a household's level of consumption because workers' disposable income will fall as they move from paid employment to the receipt of welfare benefit payments. This will mean that households affected by unemployment will cut back on consumption spending, which will result in a decrease in aggregate demand. It will also create uncertainty among working householders who may fear unemployment, which will result in them cutting back on consumption and putting more of their income into savings. This will reduce the level of demand in the economy and result in a slower rate of real GDP growth.

ℯ 4/4 marks awarded. The answer consists of correct identification of a relevant point, followed by the statement of a logical chain of reasoning to explain the point.

[03]

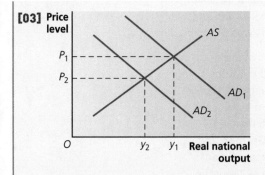

Consumption means the total planned consumer expenditure in the whole economy. It is the most important component of aggregate demand as it accounts for approximately 65% of total spending in the UK economy every year. Hence a slowdown in consumption growth will significantly affect the level of total aggregate demand and possibly result in a recession.

Macroeconomic performance can be judged according to three main indicators: economic growth, control of inflation and the rate of unemployment. A slowdown in consumption is probably going to mean that the economy falls into recession. This will be due to households demanding fewer goods and firms producing less goods and services. This will not help unemployment because demand for labour will be lower as firms cut back on production. The demand for labour is derived from the demand for products. It will help inflation though because lower demand will mean that inflationary pressures slow down. In the diagram, this is illustrated by the AD curve shifting to the left, which causes the price level to fall from P_1 to P_2. This will be good because lower prices will increase workers' purchasing power and enable them to buy more goods in the shops.

[04] Sustained economic growth is when an economy can grow at a rate which can be maintained in the long run because the productive potential of the economy has been enhanced. This is achieved by firms investing in capital goods and improving the quality of their workers' skills. Government can also enhance the productive capacity by implementing supply-side policies that improve the nation's economic infrastructure or raise the quality of workers' skills by improving education and training programmes.

The need for the UK to rebalance its economy towards trade and investment was advocated by some economists and business leaders following the Great Recession of 2008 to 2009. They argued that the UK needs to export more goods and services and reduce consumption if it is to achieve stable long-term economic growth. The UK's balance of payments position on the current account has been in persistent deficit since 1984 and in 2013 the deficit on the current account was £72.3bn. Due to the long-term forces of globalisation the UK has experienced large-scale deindustrialisation and is a net importer of goods. In 2013 the deficit in the trade in goods was £110.2bn.

If the UK is to rebalance its economy it needs to invest in its manufacturing and engineering sector. The UK cannot compete in low-end manufacturing because businesses in China have a competitive advantage in this sector. They have lower production costs because they benefit from significantly lower wage costs. Therefore, British firms need to focus on high-end manufacturing and compete in markets where American, German and Japanese firms have traditionally dominated. This requires significant investment in the quality of the productive capacity and the skills of the workforce. How effective this investment will be is questionable. German and Japanese firms have strong established brands, such as Mercedes and Lexus, and it is difficult to see a rival British firm competing for a sizeable market share in many high-end markets. Furthermore, the workforce skills and manufacturing expertise needed to build a competitive industry would take decades of expensive investment.

Long-term growth can also be achieved by developing the service sector. The UK has one of the most competitive service sectors in the world and a distinct competitive advantage in many areas. In 2013 the UK ran a trade surplus on services of £78.1bn. Rather than pursuing policies that seek to raise the performance of manufacturing firms it may be wiser for the government to focus on policies that allow service sector businesses to entrench their position as market leaders in world markets. Investment in workers' skills by focusing on the quality of education and vocational training schemes should provide firms with more of the workers that they demand. However, government spending on infrastructure projects that improve transportation, such as the building of rail networks and airports, or communications, such as ensuring that high-speed broadband is more accessible, are all polices that will encourage long-term growth.

The government may also want to consider rethinking the demand-side policies that were pursued in 2010. As Extract B says, as a result of the large 'UK fiscal consolidation in 2010 and in 2011' aggregate demand has been suppressed. George Osborne increased VAT from 17.5% to 20% and reduced the budgets of most government departments by a fifth. 'Cumulatively, the UK government tightened fiscal policy by 3% more than the US government did' (Extract B). As can be seen in the graph in Extract A, the US economy recovered more quickly than the UK economy. By the middle of 2011 the US economy had recovered from the 2008 recession while the UK economy did not recover until 2014.

If the UK economy is to experience sustained economic growth it must focus on both demand-side and supply-side policies. In the depth of a recession demand-side polices are needed to stimulate growth and set the economy on the path of recovery. However, in order to achieve long-term growth the government needs to have a sensible supply-side approach. Rebalancing towards trade is obvious but what type of rebalancing and to what sort of trade are important questions. Rather than focusing on industrial markets dominated by fierce competitors the UK must focus on what it does best: services. Hence the government should ensure that it provides the correct skills for the workforce and an infrastructure that will enable business to thrive. If the government spends on investment in transport, high-speed communications and affordable housing, it may provide a demand-side stimulus that creates sustainable low-inflation growth.

e 24/25 marks awarded. This is an excellent Part [04] answer, which easily reaches Level 5. The student introduces a significant number of explanatory and relevant points and evaluates each in turn. The final paragraph provides a good conclusion. One slight quibble is that although the meaning of sustained economic growth is explained, the meaning of rebalancing the economy, though implicit in the answer, would benefit from being made more explicit.

e Total score: 39/40 marks = Grade A*

Student B

[01] 3%

e 0/2 marks awarded. The answer lies outside the acceptable range and as the student's workings are not shown, a mark cannot be awarded for correct method but with a calculation slip along the way.

[02] One reason why the recovery in the UK was worse than in the USA was because real incomes were less in the UK than in the USA as a result of energy price increases. This would mean that British households had less money than US households so they spent less on consumption. This would have slowed GDP.

e **3/4 marks awarded.** While not being wrong, the answer needs more development, for example along the lines of the earlier Grade-A* answer. There is not enough for full marks here.

---

[03] If consumption falls then aggregate demand will shift to the left. This can be seen in the diagram. Consumption is a component of aggregate demand, so if it goes down that means that *AD* will decrease as can be seen in the formula $AD = C + I + G + (X - M)$.

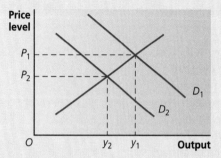

If *AD* goes down, this will be bad for economic growth because it will fall from Y_1 to Y_2. It will, however, be good for inflation because that will fall from P_1 to P_2. Employment will also go down between Y_1 and Y_2. So, overall, a slowdown in consumption will be bad because it will mean that growth and employment fall, which will lead to lower living standards, although lower inflation might be good because money will become more valuable again.

---

e **4/9 marks awarded.** Though the student shows some understanding, this is a rather sloppy answer, both in the diagram and in the written part of the answer. In the diagram, the student has failed to label the *AS* curve and has incorrectly labelled the *AD* curves, while the written answer seems to confuse, for example, a change in employment with a change in national income. More importantly, points are stated but not developed. This is a mid-Level 2 answer.

---

[04] In order to achieve long-term sustainable growth the government needs to implement supply-side polices. Supply-side polices will enhance the capacity of the economy and allow for stable growth without inflationary pressures in the economy. Investment is the key to supply-side policies and the engine of long-term growth. Investment is both a component of aggregate demand and also the reason why the structure of the economy will improve.

If the economy is to achieve sustainable economic growth it needs to invest in policies that allow it to improve its trade. By improving the quality of the goods that are made, the UK will improve its export sales. As firms make better goods they will see an improvement in sales because foreigners will want to buy the products. The first best policy for the government to pursue is supply-side policies that focus on skills and education.

The problem with most British businesses is that they struggle to find workers with the right skills. Engineering skills and technical skills are good but not enough workers have them. If more workers have them then UK firms will have better workers. This will help them to grow. Therefore, the government must focus on the supply side. It must pursue policies that enhance the standard of education and training. This will give firms the human capital that they need. This will cost billions of pounds but it will be well spent because it will be investment in the future and will result in a high rate of economic growth in the future.

The second best supply-side policy that the government needs to implement in order to encourage trade and promote growth is the cutting of 'red tape'. One of the problems that the UK has is that there are too many regulations and restrictions that prevent businesses from operating freely. For example, unnecessary health and safety regulations add costs to businesses. This means that British businesses are uncompetitive when trying to sell goods to businesses in emerging markets. The government, therefore, needs to help UK businesses cut costs and deregulate so that they can sell their products at a lower price. This will stimulate trade and result in a faster rate of economic growth.

The third best supply-side policy that the government could implement is privatisation. Private companies are better run and more efficient than public sector corporations. Private businesses are run by managers who are motivated by the profit incentive. Public sector managers lack this incentive and do not take the tough decisions that lead to dynamic companies. Therefore, to make UK firms more competitive the government needs to privatise firms. The Royal Mail was successfully privatised and now the government needs to sell its shares in RBS and Lloyds bank, and look at selling off the BBC. This will make the companies more efficient and world-leading companies that will sell their products around the world. This will create jobs and help the UK into sustained economic recovery.

(e) **13/25 marks awarded.** This is a mid-Level 3 answer (11–15 marks). It focuses rather narrowly on supply-side policies, while not discussing the fact that most supply-side policies have already been implemented in the UK for several years. They are hardly a 'magic bullet' for continuous improvement in national economic performance. Nevertheless, the answer meets the Level 3 descriptors of some reasonable analysis but generally unsupported evaluation, satisfactory knowledge and understanding of economic terminology, concepts and principles, though with some weaknesses and fairly superficial evaluation.

(e) **Total score: 20/40 marks = Grade C**

Question 3 Fiscal policy (AS)

Context 1

Total for this Context: 50 marks

Study Extracts A, B and C, and then answer all parts of Context 1 which follow.

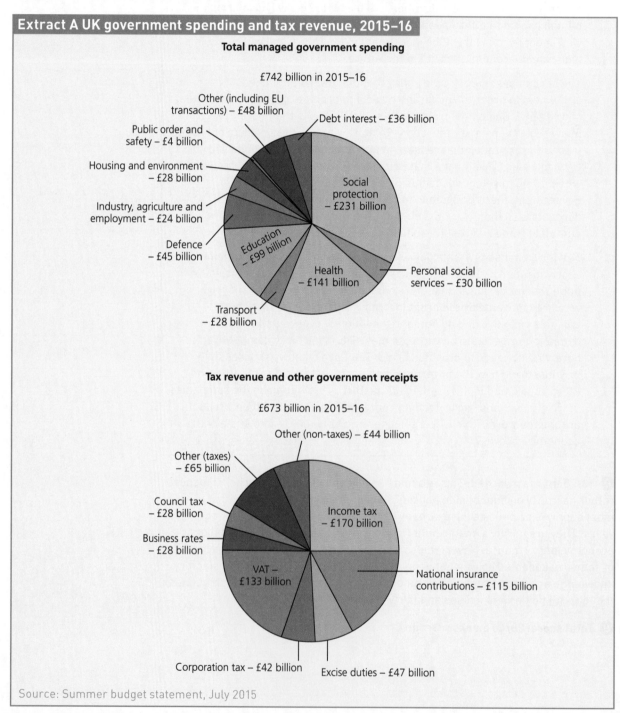

Extract A UK government spending and tax revenue, 2015–16

Total managed government spending

£742 billion in 2015–16

- Other (including EU transactions) – £48 billion
- Debt interest – £36 billion
- Public order and safety – £4 billion
- Housing and environment – £28 billion
- Industry, agriculture and employment – £24 billion
- Defence – £45 billion
- Education – £99 billion
- Social protection – £231 billion
- Health – £141 billion
- Personal social services – £30 billion
- Transport – £28 billion

Tax revenue and other government receipts

£673 billion in 2015–16

- Other (non-taxes) – £44 billion
- Other (taxes) – £65 billion
- Council tax – £28 billion
- Business rates – £28 billion
- VAT – £133 billion
- Income tax – £170 billion
- National insurance contributions – £115 billion
- Corporation tax – £42 billion
- Excise duties – £47 billion

Source: Summer budget statement, July 2015

Extract B The case for budget deficits

Macroeconomists divide into two groups: Keynesians and those of a pro-free-market persuasion. Keynesian economists, named after the famous economist John Maynard Keynes, who many regard as the founder of modern [5] macroeconomics, believe that a budget deficit performs an important function in stabilising the economic cycle. Keynesians argue that if left to itself and without macro-management by the government, the economy is prone to booms and [10] busts. But by intervening in the economy and deliberately using budget deficits and surpluses, governments can use fiscal policy to 'smooth' the path of the economic cycle. The fluctuations between 'boom' and 'bust' become milder, while [15] in the downturn of the cycle, recessions can more likely be avoided.

Indeed, governments can use the size of their budget deficits to manage the level of aggregate demand in the economy. In the downturn of an [20] economic cycle, a Keynesian-inspired government may decide to increase public sector spending and perhaps also to cut taxes in order to inject spending into the economy. Conversely, in an upswing, the government may use the opposite [25] policies so as to cut its budget deficit. By doing so, the government takes demand out of an overheated economy, once again 'smoothing' the economic cycle.

Source: News reports, 2015

Extract C The case against budget deficits

Many pro-free-market or anti-Keynesian economists believe that budget deficits lead to two evils. These are rampant inflation and the creeping growth of 'big government' in the economy. With regard to the former, they argue that budget [5] deficits lead to excess demand in the economy, which brings about demand-pull inflation.

In the context of 'big government', free-market economists believe that an increase in government spending, which creates a large [10] budget deficit, means that the public sector grows at the expense of the private sector. And since much of government spending is wealth-consuming rather than wealth-creating, by displacing economic activity from the private [15] sector to the public sector, a growing budget deficit reduces economic efficiency and makes the economy's industries less competitive in international markets.

Source: News reports, 2015

[21] Define the term 'budget deficit' (Extract B, line 6) [3 marks]

ⓔ Make sure you don't confuse a budget deficit with a balance of payments deficit.

[22] Extract A shows government spending and revenues in 2015–16.

Calculate the median item by value in the government spending chart and the median item by value in the revenues chart. [4 marks]

ⓔ A median value is a measure of an average. Make sure you don't confuse it with a mean value.

[23] Using Extract A, identify two significant features of the pattern of government spending in the UK in 2015–16. [4 marks]

ⓔ A significant feature could be identifying the most important item, both as an absolute total and as a percentage of total government spending.

[24] Lines 18–20 of Extract B state that 'governments can use the size of their budget deficits to manage the level of aggregate demand in the economy'.

Draw an aggregate demand and aggregate supply (*AD/AS*) diagram to show the effect of an increase in the size of a budget deficit on the price level and real national output. [4 marks]

ℯ Make sure you don't confuse a fall in the size of a budget deficit with an increase in its size.

[25] Lines 13–14 of Extract B state that governments can use fiscal policy to 'smooth' the path of the economic cycle.

Explain why a government may wish to 'smooth' the path of an economic cycle. [10 marks]

ℯ To reach the highest Level 3 in the levels of response to the fifth part of an AS data-response question, you should write an answer that 'is well organised and develops one or more of the key issues that are relevant to the question'. You could usefully introduce concepts not mentioned in the extract, such as the multiplier, into your answer.

[26] Extracts B and C explain some of the arguments in favour of and against budget deficits.

Using the data in the extracts and your economic knowledge, evaluate the case for and against governments running budget deficits. [25 marks]

ℯ Don't simply copy out the data in Extracts B and C. The data provide prompts that you should first identify and then develop. The best answers might also draw on your economic knowledge of points not mentioned in the extracts, for example evaluation of the impact on the UK economy of recent UK budget deficits.

Student A

[21] A budget deficit is when a government has to borrow money in order to pay for the expenditure which exceeds income received from tax revenues.

ℯ **3/3 marks awarded.** This is an accurate definition. Remember, government spending and public spending can be treated as interchangeable terms (public spending is undertaken in the public sector of the economy).

[22] The median value by spending was debt interest at £36bn; the median value by revenue was excise duties at £47bn.

ℯ **4/4 marks awarded.** Two correct answers, but just in case a slip is made in the calculation, it is best to write out all the numbers in descending or ascending order before picking out the middle number in ranking order.

[23] The first significant feature was that 30.1% of government spending was on social protection, which was the highest single area of spending. This is significant because spending on social protection (i.e. welfare benefits) is wealth-consuming rather than wealth-creating.

The second significant feature was that spending on merit goods came to £231bn.

e 2/4 marks awarded. Because the student does not explain why the second feature is significant, no marks are awarded for this point. However, 2 marks are awarded for the first point.

[24]

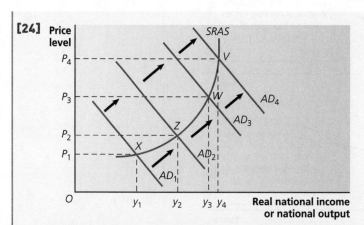

A budget deficit can increase either because G increases or because T falls. Either way, it is an injection of spending into the economy, which shifts the AD curve rightward. What happens to the price level and to the level of real output following the shift depends, first on the size of the increase in the budget deficit, and second on the slope or gradient of the $SRAS$ curve. My diagram shows three shifts of the AD curve. The first shift, from AD_1 to AD_2, causes both the price level and real output to increase, but the proportionate change in real output is greater than the proportionate change in the price level. This might be because the economy is initially in deep recession, with lots of spare capacity that can be brought into production to meet the increase in demand. By contrast, if the AD curve is initially AD_3, the economy is close to full employment and the 'normal' capacity level of output. The lack of spare capacity means that the $SRAS$ curve is nearly vertical. In this situation, the shift of AD from AD_3 to AD_4 will result mostly in inflation. Excess demand pulls up the price level in a demand-pull inflation. Real output does, however, increase to a certain extent, but if the $SRAS$ curve was vertical, there would be no long-term increase in real output.

e 4/4 marks awarded. This is an excellent answer in all respects except one — it is over-long. The fact that the question has a maximum mark of 4 means that only about 8 minutes should be spent writing an answer (2 minutes a mark).

[25] A government will seek to smooth the path of an economic cycle because the economy is 'prone to booms and busts', which can cause undesirable problems in an economy. A government will run large budget deficits in a recession to stimulate aggregate demand and avoid the recession sinking into a deep depression. In a boom a government will run a contractionary fiscal policy, which cuts spending and raises taxation to cool the economy and avoid speculative booms. The contractionary fiscal policy may allow the government to run a budget surplus, which can be used to pay off part of the national debt.

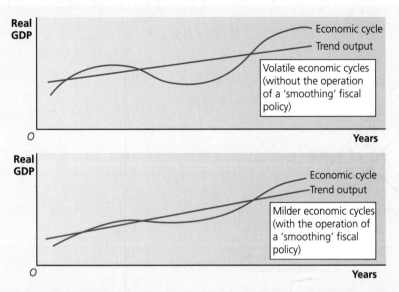

A government will want to intervene in a recession primarily to prevent the collapse of industries perceived to be too important to fail and mass unemployment. In the 2007/08 banking crisis the government spent billions of pounds and ran massive budget deficits (up to 14% of GDP), partly to prevent large banks, such as RBS and HBOS, from going bust. This was considered necessary to prevent an even bigger crisis and a deeper recession. In November 2008 the government cut VAT to 15% in order to stimulate consumer spending and help businesses stay solvent. This helped many businesses avoid bankruptcy and unemployment reaching the 3 million level seen in the recessions in the early 1980s and 1990s.

A government will justify this action on the grounds that it will reduce volatility in the economy and create greater macroeconomic stability. This will be good for consumer and business confidence, which should create an environment for households to plan their expenditure and firms to invest in capital equipment without fear.

ⓔ **10/10 marks awarded.** This is an excellent answer, which we have placed at the top of Level 3, the highest level for the penultimate part of an AS DRQ.

[26] A budget deficit is when a government needs to borrow money in a financial year because its revenue from taxation and other revenue sources does not cover its spending commitments. In a modern economy it is inevitable that a government will run a budget deficit in a recession but the size of the deficit and the policies that a government pursues vary. Economists can be divided into two main camps. Keynesian economists argue that in a recession a government should run large budget deficits and stimulate economic growth. In contrast, free-market economists argue that governments need to implement policies that reduce the budget deficit as quickly as possible and run surpluses to pay down the national debt sooner rather than later.

The Keynesian macroeconomic approach aims to run large budget deficits during a recession, which has the function of 'stabilising the economic cycle' (Extract B). Keynesian economists believe that if the government does not inject spending into the economy a deep recession or even a depression will set in. Household and business confidence will collapse and the level of aggregate demand will fall significantly. This will result in high unemployment, poverty will increase and average living standards will fall. Keynesian economists believe that with government 'macro-management' (Extract B) the economy is prone to demand deficiency and will operate below capacity. Therefore the government must run a large budget deficit in order to stimulate aggregate demand. Government spending is a component of *AD* so by increasing spending in the economy, aggregate demand will be stimulated. This will take the form of 'increased public sector spending' (Extract B) and should create positive multiplier effects. This is when an injection of spending has positive knock-on effects in the economy. For example, an increase in spending on road building will increase demand for tarmac and concrete, which will lead to jobs being created in quarries. The workers employed both directly and indirectly by the government will have a higher level of disposable income, which they will spend in retail centres shopping and eating out. This will create demand for goods and services and lead to the employment of more workers.

Budget deficits will therefore create growth and maintain a reasonable level of employment in a recession which will benefit the economy significantly. As the economy recovers the deficits will be reduced and in time the level of government spending will be reduced. The recovery will also see increasing employment which should result in higher taxation revenues. This will enable the government to run a series of budget surpluses and pay down the national debt.

Free-market economists are wary of budget deficits although they do believe that it is necessary to run a deficit in a deep recession. Chancellor George Osborne has adopted many of the policies advocated by pro-market economists but he does not plan to eliminate the UK's budget deficit until 2020. Moreover, under his Charter for Budget Responsibility, the government can still run deficits during an economic crisis.

Pro-market economists reject Keynesian theory because they do not believe that a government can spend its way out of a recession. They argue that when a government runs a large budget deficit it will lead to government spending that is 'wealth-consuming rather than wealth-creating' (Extract C). The government will spend money on public sector projects that create jobs but do not significantly improve the infrastructure of the economy or improve economic efficiency. In the long run this spending will have to be paid back, which will require taxation on wealth-creating private enterprises. Hence, large budget deficits have the long-term effect of 'displacing economic activity from the private sector to the public sector' (Extract C).

Most Keynesian and pro-free-market economists are agreed that in a recession the government should allow a budget deficit to occur, because in a downturn, tax revenues automatically fall and welfare spending automatically rises. Keynesians believe that large deficits are desirable because the government needs to stabilise economic activity. Pro-market economists believe that governments need to control spending and quickly reduce the size of the deficit in a crisis. Either way all governments should run a deficit in a recession.

ⓔ **15/25 marks awarded.** Although this answer shows good understanding of quite difficult concepts and is well presented, we have decided to place it at the top of Level 3 (11–15 marks), which means that overall the script earns a low A grade. We are unwilling to place the answer any higher because the student largely regurgitates the content of Extracts B and C, with some additional explanation. Evaluation is thin, because the student does not address sufficiently the key requirement of the question, namely to evaluate the case for and against governments running budget deficits.

ⓔ **Total score: 38/50 marks = Grade A**

Student B

[21] A budget deficit is when government borrows money by selling bonds, and when $G \rightarrow T$.

ⓔ **3/3 marks awarded.** The first part of the answer earns no marks because it states a possible consequence of a budget deficit rather than a definition. However, the statement that $G \rightarrow T$ in the second part of the answer picks up all 3 marks.

[22] Debt interest and excise duties were the median values.

ⓔ **3/4 marks awarded.** The correct answers are given but 1 mark is lost because the numbers are not quoted. Apart from that, the same comment applies as that made for the Student A answer.

[23] Over a quarter of the government's budget was spent on social protection. Industry, agriculture and employment was the department that the government spent the least money on.

ⓔ **0/4 marks awarded.** The student does not explain why the two points made are significant, and no numbers are quoted as evidence .Stating that spending on social protection is just over a quarter of total government spending is not enough to gain a mark.

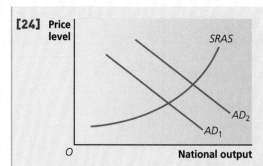

[24]

My diagram shows the *AD* curve shifting to the right. Both the price level and real output would change.

ⓔ 1/4 marks awarded. The diagram is fine as far as it goes but the coordinates, which would show what happens to the price level and real output, have not been drawn. Taking the diagram and the written answer together, 1 mark is awarded.

[25] The government will 'smooth' the economic cycle by using deficits and surpluses to control the business cycle. In a recession the government will run a deficit. This means that it will put money into the economy. It will do this so that it creates spending, which will help the economy come out of a bust. When the government runs a deficit it will borrow money from the markets. This money will need to be paid back at a later date. Budget deficits are an economic flow and are measured on an annual basis. The deficits go into the national debt, which is an economic stock. If the government's national debt gets too high it could create a debt crisis. This has happened to Greece in recent years.

The government will run a surplus when it wants to stop the economy from going into a boom. It will do this by cutting government spending and increasing taxation. This will take spending out of the economy. Higher taxation will mean that households have less disposable income so they will cut consumption. A higher rate of corporation tax will mean that firms have less money for investment. Three major components of aggregate demand will fall and the level of GDP will decrease. This is how a government will smooth the economic cycle.

ⓔ 7/10 marks awarded. The answer displays a reasonable understanding of the concepts relevant to the question. Analysis is reasonable and mistake-free, but it needs more development. The answer is placed at the top of Level 2 (4–7 marks).

[26] Keynesians say that governments should run budget deficits and surpluses to control the economy. They think that it is a good thing for the government to control the economy and achieve its macroeconomic objects: economic growth, full employment, stable prices and balance of payments equilibrium in the long run. Extract B says 'if left to itself and without macro-management by the government, the economy is prone to booms and busts'. This is bad and therefore the government should borrow money in an economic downturn to get out of recession.

When the government borrows money and spends it in the economy this means that aggregate demand will increase. Government spending is a component of *AD* so the curve will shift to the right. This will increase economic growth but it will also create demand-pull inflation. Economic growth is good because it means the economy is growing. Inflation is bad because it means that money is losing its value and households have reduced purchasing power. This is a trade-off the Keynesians have to make and they choose to have higher growth and higher inflation.

Free-market economists disagree with Keynesian economists. They believe that inflation is bad and that this is caused by budget deficits. This also is bad because it leads to big government. Extract C describes this situation as being a twin evil. This is a major problem because it means that prices go up and the government employs more civil servants. This may create more jobs but it means that more government officials get in the way of business and do not do very much.

Another problem with borrowing money is that the government will one day have to pay it back. This is a problem because debt can be seen as wrong because the government has to pay interest on the debt it has. Therefore the government needs to pay off the debt and run budget surpluses.

Keynesian economists may want to save the economy but they will do this by spending money that they have borrowed. This needs to be paid back with interest and is a problem. Free-market economists believe that deficits are bad and that the government should pay off its debts. This makes more sense because the government needs to balance its budget.

e **12/25 marks awarded.** In contrast to the Student A answer, this is placed at the bottom of Level 3 rather than any higher up. The answer reaches some but not all of the Level 3 descriptors. Those that are met are: some application of relevant economic principles and, where appropriate, some use of data to support the response; inadequately developed analysis and fairly superficial evaluation; with some attempt to make relevant judgements but these are not well supported by arguments and/or data.

e **Total score: 26/50 marks = Grade C**

Question 4 Inflation and deflation (A-level)

Context 1

Total for this Context: 40 marks

Study Extracts A, B and C, and then answer all parts of Context 1 which follow.

Extract A The UK consumer prices index (CPI) and indices for selected items used in the construction of the CPI, August 2013 to August 2015

	Food and non-alcoholic beverages	Clothing and footwear	Housing, water, electricity, gas and other fuels	Furniture, household equipment and routine maintenance	Transport	CPI (overall index)
	Weights					
2015	110	70	128	59	149	1000
	Monthly indices (2005 = 100)					
2013 Aug	144.2	80.4	150.5	119.9	138.9	126.4
2014 Aug	142.6	80.7	155.3	120.3	140.5	128.3
2015 Aug	139.2	81.2	155.9	128.8	136.8	128.3
	Percentage change on a year					
2013 Aug	4.1	1.6	4.2	1.1	1.2	2.7
2014 Aug	−1.1	0.4	3.2	0.4	1.2	1.5
2015 Aug	−2.4	0.6	0.4	0.4	−2.6	0

Source: ONS, September 2015

Extract B 'Good' and 'bad' deflations

Deflation can be bad as well as good. 'Bad' deflations are caused by a collapse of aggregate demand. When people believe prices are going to fall, they postpone 'big ticket' consumption decisions, for example replacing their cars. [5] Consumers acquire a deflationary mentality and stop spending. As a result the economy stagnates.

A 'good' deflation results from improvements in the economy's supply side which reduce businesses' costs of production. In 2015 world raw [10] material prices and oil prices have been falling. However, this may not be as good as it seems because the falling prices may have been caused by slower growth in China, the world's major consumer of industrial raw materials. Events in [15] the world economy such as a worldwide recession might result in a fall in the global demand for British exports. This could trigger a 'bad' deflation in the UK.

Source: News reports, 2015

Extract C Inflation and deflation in the UK

If inflation is generally seen to be bad, its opposite, deflation or a falling price level, must surely be good, both for the performance of the economy and for individuals. But is this necessarily so?

The main measure of UK inflation, the Consumer [5] Prices Index, turned negative in April 2015, with the inflation rate falling to −0.1%. The index showed that transport costs were 2.8% lower in April than the same time in 2014, while food was 3.0% cheaper. A falling price level meant that a [10] basket of goods and services that cost £100 in April 2014 would have cost £99.90 in April 2015.

Chancellor George Osborne said the negative inflation figure should not be mistaken for a →

'damaging deflation'. He added that the lower cost of living — driven by last year's fall in oil prices — would be a welcome relief for family budgets, in an environment in which average wages were finally beginning to rise.

Does the April figure mean that deflation has arrived in Britain? Many economists believe that the answer is 'no'. This is because 'core' inflation, a measure which excludes transitory or temporary price volatility as in the case of some commodities, food items and energy prices, has remained positive at about 1%. Economists also argue that 'proper' deflation is a *long-term* trend of declining prices, and they believe that current price falls won't endure much more than a month or two — though in the odd month the price level may occasionally fall.

Source: News reports, 2015

[01] Using the data in Extract A, calculate to two decimal places the percentage change in average prices of food and non-alcoholic beverages between August 2013 and August 2015.

[2 marks]

ⓔ The data is presented in index number form, with a base index number of 100 in 2005. Percentages also add up to 100, so make sure you don't confuse index numbers with percentages.

[02] Explain how the weights allocated to the different selected items of consumer spending shown in Extract A help in the construction of the UK consumer prices index.

[4 marks]

ⓔ When answering this question, take note of the fact that Extract A does not include all the items and all the weights used in the construction of the CPI. Some items, such as spending on health and education, are missing.

[03] Line 1 of Extract B states: 'Deflation can be bad as well as good.'

With the aid of an *AD/AS* diagram, explain how a 'bad' deflation is caused.

[9 marks]

ⓔ This question requires the use of an *AD/AS* diagram. Extract B gives several prompts on the shifts of *AD* and *AS* curves that can cause the price level to fall. Make sure you identify the correct shift that illustrates a 'bad' deflation.

[04] Lines 1–4 of Extract C state: 'If inflation is generally seen to be bad, its opposite, deflation or a falling price level, must be good, both for the performance of the economy and for individuals.'

Using the data in the extracts and your economic knowledge, evaluate the case for the UK government replacing the current 2% CPI inflation target with a 0% CPI inflation target.

[25 marks]

ⓔ Although the question asks for an evaluation of the 'case for', a good answer will also explain the 'case against' and evaluate both. A very good A-level answer might also consider replacing inflation targets with some other target, e.g. a nominal GDP target, an employment target or a growth target, or completely dropping any form of targeting.

Student A

[01] −5/144.2 x 100 = −3.47%. Between August 2013 and August 2015, the price index for food and non-alcoholic beverages fell by 5 index points. Minus 5 as a ratio of the August 2015 price index of 144.2, converted into a percentage, represents a change in the price index of −3.47%, taken to two decimal places.

ⓔ **2/2 marks awarded.** A perfect answer, hence full marks.

[02] Because people spend more on some goods than on others, a 5% fall in the price of petrol would have a much bigger impact on the CPI than a similar percentage fall in the price of biscuits. For this reason, the components of the index are 'weighted' to ensure that it reflects the importance of the various items in the average shopping basket. Without an accurate system of weighting, the overall CPI would not measure accurately changes in the average price level.

ⓔ **4/4 marks awarded.** Again, a perfect answer.

[03]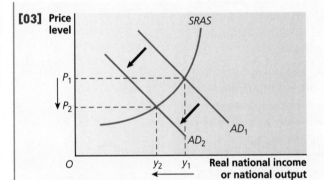

Bad deflation, also known as malign deflation, is when the price level turns negative because there has been a collapse in aggregate demand in the economy. This is a very serious economic problem that can result in the collapse of business confidence, firms significantly cutting back on investment and production, and mass unemployment.

Bad deflation will normally set in during a recession caused by a major economic crisis. As a consequence of the downturn households will cut back on consumption spending. Demand for goods and services will fall and businesses will respond by cutting production. In turn, firms will require fewer hours to be worked, which may result in redundancies or it may lead to underemployment as workers are offered less work and accept lower wages. Either way levels of disposable income fall and households respond by cutting back on consumption. Firms respond by cutting back on production and aggregate demand decreases further.

Bad deflation is a major problem because once it sets in households and firms can fall into a mindset that is difficult to break. The downward spiral will be made worse when firms postpone investment projects and unemployed workers forget their skills and become less employable.

e **5/9 marks awarded.** The written part of the answer is good and of Level 3 quality. However, because the *AD/AS* diagram, though accurate, is not linked to the written part, the answer is placed in mid-Level 2 (4–6 marks).

[04] Official rule-based inflation targeting has been central to UK monetary policy since 1997. The chancellor of the exchequer sets a 2% inflation target measured by the CPI, which the MPC seeks to achieve in the long run by using monetary policy to manage aggregate demand. The policy framework is widely seen as having been one of the best economic achievements in the last 20 years but since the Great Recession there have been strong arguments put forward to reform the system.

Economists that advocate replacing the existing 2% target with a 0% target see inflation as being the biggest problem facing an economy. They see the hyper-inflation that took place in Germany in the early 1920s and immediately after the Second World War in the 1940s as being extremely dangerous, because it led to great economic instability and political turmoil. Inflation is the persistent rise in average prices and if it is allowed to set in then it erodes the value of money. This undermines household confidence and results in the transfer of wealth from savers to debtors. They argue that the government should seek to eliminate inflation and build a strong economy based on stability and confidence.

The problem with this approach is that it does not pay enough attention to the problem of deflation, or the benefits of inflation. Deflation is when average prices are falling and the purchasing power of the average household is increasing. As Extract B states, 'deflation can be bad as well as good'. Falling prices may sound good, but if this is due to a collapse in the level of aggregate demand it could be extremely harmful. This is known as malign deflation. This sets in when a recession takes hold of an economy and households and businesses lose confidence because they fear the future. Households will cut back on expenditure and postpone 'big ticket' (Extract B) purchases, such as new cars. This leads to firms cutting back on production. They may also ask their workers to become more flexible with their hours, accept pay cuts or make redundancies.

In this situation monetary policy needs to be loose and seek to stimulate aggregate demand. The problem with a 0% target is that policy-makers may leave it too late to act. They may fear that if they act too quickly and cut rates this will result in inflation higher than is acceptable. Hence they will hold off until it is too late and allow a deflationary mindset to set into the economy.

The 0% target will also be bad because it does not take into account the benefits of inflation. While a high level of inflation is undesirable a low rate of inflation allows firms to cut real wages without cutting nominal wages. This is achieved when a firm offers workers a pay rise below the rate of inflation. If inflation is at 2% then firms offer a 1% pay rise. Nominal pay goes up but in real terms workers' wages have fallen. This allows firms to make pay cuts. It also encourages workers to spend their wages knowing that if they keep their savings in cash it will be slowly lose its value.

In conclusion, there are good arguments for reforming the current monetary policy system but changing the target to 0% inflation is not one of them. This will create a deflationary bias in the setting of monetary policy, which will suppress demand and could result in the lost decade of stagnant economic growth seen in Japan in the 1990s. If the targeting system is to be changed then perhaps policy-makers should consider asking the MPC to consider the importance of long-term economic growth, the performance of the UK housing market or the level of unemployment. These are extremely important areas of macroeconomic performance that need to be considered.

e **21/25 marks awarded.** This answer is placed at the lower end of Level 5. It meets the Level 5 descriptor of 'sound, focused analysis and well-supported evaluation'. The answer is well organised, showing sound knowledge and understanding of economic terminology, concepts and principles with few errors. It includes good application of relevant economic principles and relevant use of the text data, though not of the numerical data, in the extracts. The conclusion is a bit of an afterthought. It would be better to discuss the pros and cons of alternatives to inflation targeting in more depth earlier in the answer.

e **Total score: 32/40 marks = Grade A**

Student B
[01] 3.476

e **0/2 marks awarded.** Although on first sight the number appears to be correct, the minus sign has been omitted, the answer is not expressed to two decimal points and the percentage sign is missing.

[02] The weights used in the construction of a price index reflect the relative importance of each item.

e **3/4 marks awarded.** While not being wrong, the answer needs more development, for example along the lines of the earlier Student A answer. There is not enough for full marks here.

[03]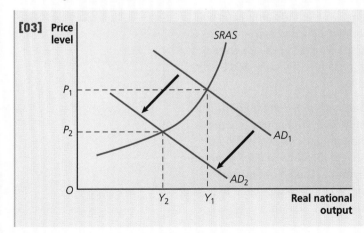

A bad deflation, illustrated on my diagram above, is caused by a collapse in aggregate demand, usually when the economy enters recession with real GDP falling for at least two quarters. The bad deflation is caused by whatever factors led to the collapse in aggregate demand. Two possibilities are a collapse of consumer confidence and a collapse of business confidence. Back in the 1930s, John Maynard Keynes talked about a collapse in businessmen's 'animal spirits', i.e. their gut feeling about the poor outlook facing the economy. Other possible causes of a collapse in aggregate demand could be a collapse of demand for the country's exports, itself related to importing recession from the rest of the world. There is an old saying: 'when America sneezes, the rest of the world catches a cold'. While still relevant today, more recent possibilities are catching recession from China or from events in the eurozone, which then lead into a bad recession in the UK.

ⓔ **7/9 marks awarded.** This is a good answer, but to earn full marks the student should provide a better link between the diagram and the written part of the answer.

[04] Inflation can be defined as the erosion of the value of money, which means that consumers can buy fewer goods and services for their money. This is a problem because it means that high inflation will reduce living standards and it is why the control of inflation is the government's main macroeconomic objective.

Inflation in the UK is measured by the CPI index, which is a shopping basket of products bought by the average British household. It makes sense for the government to reduce the target rate of inflation to 0% from its current rate of 2% because it would be better for households and firms to benefit from lower prices. As Extract C states, between April 2014 and 2015 the average cost of a basket of goods actually fell from £100 to £99.90. This may only be a gain of 10 pence but it means that the average household has a higher level of disposable income, which is a good thing.

The problem with the 2% target is that it can allow inflation to seep into the UK economy. This can create expectations of higher inflation in the economy to take hold. If this happens, households and firms will start behaving in a manner that creates higher inflation in the future. This will lead to a rapid increase in inflationary pressures, which might lead to hyper-inflation. This would erode the value of money and lead to tremendous instability and economic chaos.

Even if high inflation does not lead to hyper-inflation, it is still bad. This is because the high inflation will create instability and annoy business leaders. They will be unhappy with the changing prices and will hold back on investment plans. If they do not invest it will be bad for economic growth and might create higher unemployment. This might be good because investment is a component of aggregate demand and if it does not increase then there will not be any demand-pull inflation.

> Ultimately inflation is bad because it erodes the value of money and creates economic uncertainty. If it sets in and expectations of future inflation take hold then it can lead to high levels of economic instability. This is really bad and will destroy long-term economic growth, which will significantly harm the economy.

ⓔ 12/25 marks awarded. The answer is sufficiently focused on the question to reach Level 3, for which the level descriptor is 'some reasonable analysis but generally unsupported evaluation'. The answer contains a number of assertions that are not properly explained or analysed, for example the statement that 'high inflation will reduce living standards' without the statement being justified. However, late in the answer the student suggests that economic instability is a link in a chain of reasoning. Overall, the answer includes some reasonable analysis together with fairly superficial evaluation, but not enough of either skill to take the answer above the midpoint in Level 3 (11–15 marks). It shows some sound knowledge but the student does not sufficiently address the question or develop some of the points made into sufficiently long chains of reasoning.

ⓔ **Total score: 22/40 marks = Grade C**

Question 5 The UK balance of payments on current account (AS)

Context 1

Total for this Context: 50 marks

Study Extracts A, B and C, and then answer all parts of Context 1 which follow.

Extract A UK balance of payments, 2014 (£ million)	
Exports of goods	292,204
Imports of goods	413,419
Exports of services	215,020
Imports of services	129,029
Balance of trade in goods and services	?
Primary income	−44,976
Secondary income	−25,451
Balance of payments on the current account	**−105,651**

Source: United Kingdom Quarterly Accounts, Quarter 1 2015, ONS

Extract B What is the current account?

The UK's current account is a measure of the transactions it conducts with the rest of the world. It is calculated by adding to the balance of trade things like the flows of money we send abroad, and income earned by UK residents on their foreign assets. The [5] last time we came close to registering anything near a surplus on the current account was back in 1997.

In fact, in the current recovery from recession, our balance of payments deficit has actually grown from 1.7% of GDP in 2011, to over 4% in [10] 2013, and then to over 5% in 2014.

Source: News reports, 2014

Extract C Do current account deficits or surpluses matter?

While a short-run deficit or surplus on current account does not pose a problem, a persistent or long-run imbalance is another matter. In the case of a deficit, the nature of any resulting problem depends on the size and cause of the deficit: the larger the [5] deficit, the greater the problem is likely to be.

A current account deficit indicates that the country's citizens are living beyond their means, enjoying in the short run a standard of living boosted by imports of goods produced in other countries. [10]

A deficit may also reflect the uncompetitiveness of the country's industries. Other countries may be more productive and capable of producing better-quality goods and services. The deficit may herald the decline of living standards within the country [15] in the future.

While many people agree that a persistent current account deficit can pose serious problems, few realise that a balance of payments surplus on current account can also lead to problems. [20] Because a surplus is often seen as a sign of national economic virility and success, a popular view is that the bigger the surplus, the better must be the country's economic performance. This is obviously true insofar as growth of the surplus reflects the [25]

growing competitiveness of the country's exporting industries. However, although a small surplus may be a justifiable objective of government policy, a large payments surplus should be regarded as undesirable. This is for two reasons: [30]

In the first place, one country's surplus is another country's deficit. Since we don't trade with Mars or any other planet, the balance of payments must balance for the world as a whole. It is therefore impossible for all countries to run surpluses [35] simultaneously. Unless countries with persistently large surpluses agree to take action to reduce their surpluses, deficit countries cannot reduce their deficits. Deficit countries may then be forced to impose import controls from which all countries, [40] including surplus countries, eventually suffer.

In the second place, a balance of payments surplus on current account increases the level of aggregate demand in the economy. This can be inflationary. If there are substantial unemployed [45] resources in the economy, this can have the beneficial effect of reflating real output and jobs. However, if the economy is initially close to full capacity, demand-pull inflation results.

Source: News reports, 2015

[21] Define the term 'recession' (Extract B, line 8). [3 marks]

ⓔ Different countries have different definitions of recessions. Any reasonable definition will do, even if it differs from the technical definition used in the UK.

[22] Extract A shows the UK balance of payments on current account for 2014, published at the end of Quarter 1 in 2015.

Calculate the value of the balance of trade in goods and services. [4 marks]

ⓔ Always look to see if the data are for £ millions or £ billions.

[23] Using Extract A, identify two significant features of the UK's balance of payments on current account in 2014. [4 marks]

e A significant feature could relate to the current account as a whole, or to an individual item in the current account.

[24] Lines 42–44 of Extract C state that 'a balance of payments surplus on current account increases the level of aggregate demand in the economy'.

Use an aggregate demand and aggregate supply (*AD/AS*) diagram to show how a balance of payments surplus on current account may affect the UK economy. [4 marks]

e You must understand that a balance of payments surplus on current account is an injection into the circular flow of income.

[25] Lines 8–11 of Extract B state that 'in the current recovery from recession, our balance of payments deficit has actually grown from 1.7% of GDP in 2011, to over 4% in 2013'.

Explain TWO ways in which an increasing deficit on the current account of the balance of payments may pose problems for the UK economy. [10 marks]

e Although the quote in the preamble to the question is taken from Extract B, the prompts that might help you to answer the question are in Extract C.

[26] Lines 19–20 of Extract C state that 'a balance of payments surplus on current account can also lead to problems'.

Using the data in the extracts and your economic knowledge, discuss whether a government should aim to achieve a balance of payments surplus on current account. [25 marks]

e To reach the highest Level 5 in the mark scheme for the last part of a Context DRQ, which asks for evaluation, you must include a 'winding up' concluding paragraph that assesses the strengths and weaknesses of the arguments introduced earlier in the answer.

Student A

[21] In the UK a recession is defined as two successive quarters of negative GDP output.

e **3/3 marks awarded.** The answer provides the 'official' definition of a recession of the UK government, though other countries, notably the USA, use other definitions of a recession.

[22] The balance of trade in goods and services equals (exported goods + exported services) – (imported goods – imported services).

For 2014, this is (£292,204 + £215,020) – (£413,419 + £129,029), which is (£507,224 – £542,448), which equals –£35,224m.

ⓔ **4/4 marks awarded.** The calculation is correct with the final minus sign indicated.

> **[23]** The first significant feature is that the largest single component of the UK's balance of payments was imported goods which were −£413,419m, and significantly higher than any other flow into or out of the economy.
>
> The second significant feature was that in 2014 the UK was running a deficit on the current account of −£105,651m, which is a large leakage of spending power leaving the UK economy.

ⓔ **4/4 marks awarded.** Both of the chosen features are significant and both are backed up with accurate statistical data, so all 4 marks are earned.

[24]

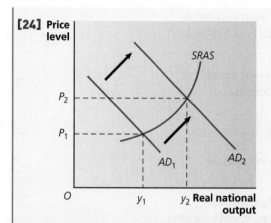

A balance of payments surplus on current account is an injection of spending into the economy's circular flow of income, and it also shifts the aggregate demand curve for output to the right. This is shown in my diagram. This stimulates or reflates real output (from y_1 to y_2) and it may also cause the price level to rise (from P_1 to P_2). The latter is likely to be the dominant effect as the *SRAS* curve becomes steeper, when the economy approaches full employment.

ⓔ **4/4 marks awarded.** This is an excellent answer that earns full marks. The written part is perhaps a little on the long side, given that only 4 marks are available for the question.

[25] A deficit on the current account of the balance of payments means that a 'country's citizens are living beyond their means' (Extract C). This means that more money is leaving the economy than entering it. The first reason why this is a problem for the UK economy is that it suggests that the UK's industries are 'uncompetitive' (Extract C).

This is a problem for the UK because it means that consumers in both the UK and abroad believe that UK products are too highly priced and/or are inferior when compared with their international competitors. If British firms struggle to sell their goods, this will lead to lower profits and slower GDP growth. Lower profits will mean that British firms will have less finance available for investing in new capital equipment. Slower GDP growth will harm economic performance and may lead to fewer jobs being created in the future.

The second reason why this may pose a problem for the UK is that the rest of the world may eventually decide not to finance the UK's current account deficit. If this happens, the supply of pounds on foreign exchange markets to finance the purchase of imports will not be matched by an equal demand for pounds. The excess supply of pounds will cause the £'s exchange rate to fall, which causes the prices of imports to rise, which might lead to the problem of cost-push inflation.

ⓔ 10/10 marks awarded. Once again, this is an excellent response that easily meets the top Level 3 descriptor with the answer 'well organised and develops one or more of the key issues that are relevant to the question, shows sound knowledge and understanding of relevant economic terminology, concepts and principles, and includes good application of relevant economic principles and/or good use of data to support the response'. A logical chain of reasoning is clearly developed.

[26] Economies that have run current account surpluses in recent years, such as China and Germany, have been associated with strong GDP growth, high levels of employment and rising living standards. Their economic success has been built on a strong manufacturing sector that exports goods across the world. China has flooded Western markets with cheap but good value goods such as lawnmowers and affordable clothing. Germany has focused on high quality engineering and boasts some of the most successful car brands in the world.

By injecting demand into the domestic economy, large current account surpluses will lead to strong GDP growth, which is desirable for a government. If domestic firms are successfully exporting their products they will be in receipt of lucrative sales revenues and profits. Chinese goods have sold well because they are cheaper than competitor products, while German goods are demanded because of their high quality and luxury status. Demand for exports should lead firms to employ more workers so that they can increase production. As firms recruit more workers it should mean that unemployment levels fall. This has occurred in China where industrialisation has created a healthy manufacturing sector, which has created hundreds of millions of jobs and lifted over 50% of the population out of absolute poverty. Germany has also experienced high levels of employment but because of its industries' focus on high quality goods the benefits of economic success have mainly been felt by workers with the skills to work for firms that are producing desirable products. Nonetheless, in both China and Germany the economies have grown because demand for their products has resulted in export-led growth and higher levels of employment. This has led to many countries wanting to replicate this strategy and build a strong economic model based on current account surpluses.

However, running a surplus can cause wider economic problems. As Extract C states, 'one country's surplus is another country's deficit'. China and Germany may be experiencing high levels of export-led growth but this means that other countries, such as the USA and UK, must be running current account deficits. Short-run surpluses and deficits are not a problem, but if they continue into the long run they are. This is because if one country is persistently exporting to run a surplus, another country must be persistently borrowing to run a deficit. It is 'impossible for all countries to run surpluses simultaneously' (Extract C). Hence if a government seeks to run persistent surpluses it will cause imbalances in the global economy, which result in deficit countries running up high levels of debt that they will struggle to pay back. This will not be in the long-term interests of a government running persistent surpluses because if one country experiences a debt crisis it is likely to create an international economic crisis that affects all countries.

A second reason why persistent deficits may be a problem is that they may result in inflationary pressures building up in an economy. Although export-led growth is desirable because it will stimulate GPD growth and increase the level of employment, this can also cause 'demand-pull inflation' (Extract C). China has experienced this problem in recent years as high levels of employment and disposable household income have resulted in food and energy prices rapidly increasing. This is a problem if it means that household purchasing power is reduced because prices are rising. Export-led growth may create more jobs but if workers do not enjoy increased living standards they will benefit from a current account surplus in the long run.

In conclusion, rather than pursuing a policy of constant current account surpluses a government would be wiser to aim for long-run equilibrium in which the current account more or less balances from year to year. This would mean that in the short run it could run both small surpluses and deficits. A surplus will result in strong GDP growth and increased employment. A deficit should result in higher living standards and a fall in inflationary pressures. Moreover, this policy will also allow other countries to run current account surpluses and pay off debts that they will have incurred during a few years of trade deficit. This will lead to a more balanced global economy and more sustainable economic growth.

ⓔ **23/25 marks awarded.** This excellent answer meets the Level 5 requirement of sound, focused analysis and well-supported evaluation. The answer is well organised, and shows sound knowledge and understanding of economic terminology, concepts and principles. There are no errors and the evaluation that runs through the answer, though it could be debated, is articulate and strong.

ⓔ **Total score: 48/50 marks = Grade A**

Student B

[21] A recession is when the UK has one quarter of negative economic growth.

ⓔ 1/3 **marks awarded.** The definition is wrong, but 1 mark has been awarded for getting the general idea of a recession.

[22] In 2014, the balance of payments deficit was –£35,224m.

ⓔ 3/4 **marks awarded.** The number is correct but it is called the balance of payments deficit on current account rather than the balance of trade deficit. Although trade flows (exports and imports) are the two major items in the current account, the current account is wider than the balance of trade, comprising primary and secondary income flows as well as trade flows. 1 mark is docked for this mistake.

[23] On the export side of the net export demand equation (X – M), the UK economy was exporting more goods than it was exporting services. It was exporting £292,204 worth of goods but only exporting £215,020 worth of services.

On the import side of the equation, the UK was importing more goods than services.

ⓔ 3/4 **marks awarded.** We have given the student the benefit of the doubt on whether the two features identified are 'significant'. You must always remember to select significant rather than random and/or trivial features of the data. Given the benefit of the doubt, the answer earns 2 marks for identifying two features and 1 mark for statistical back-up. (There is no back-up of the second feature.)

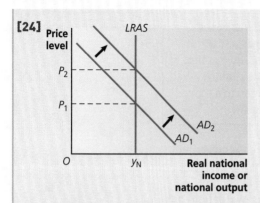

[24]

The balance of payments surplus shifts the *AD* curve rightward from AD_1 to AD_2, which leads to a greater quantity of a good being produced.

ⓔ **4/4 marks awarded.** Although this is an unexpected diagram, it still earns full marks. The diagram is unexpected because it shows the *AD* curve shifting rightward along a vertical *LRAS* curve rather than an upward-sloping *SRAS* curve. The *LRAS* curve shows the economy producing the economy's 'normal capacity' level of output, which is at or close to the full employment level of output. In this situation, the increase in aggregate demand that results from the current account surplus is inflationary rather than reflationary. This is likely when there is little or no spare productive capacity in the economy.

[25] A current account deficit is a problem for the UK government because it means that there is a shortfall between taxation revenues and government spending. This means that the government has to borrow money in order to finance the debt. In 2014 the budget deficit was £105,651m. This has occurred because the UK is living beyond its means. British consumers are buying too many goods from abroad because they are cheaper and better quality than the UK alternatives. This means that the British need money to pay for what they have spent and government needs to pay off the debts.

The current account deficit means that UK-made goods are not as good as foreign-made goods. 'Other countries may be more productive and capable of producing better-quality goods and services' (Extract C). This means that British firms are not very good and may shut down because overseas firms are better at making things. If this happens there will be mass unemployment and a deep recession.

ⓔ **2/10 marks awarded.** The first paragraph in the answer earns no marks. This is because the student has confused a balance of payments deficit on current account with a budget deficit. Many generally weaker students make this mistake. You must make sure you don't fall into this trap. However, the second paragraph is relevant to the question, which means that the answer, taken as a whole, is placed in Level 1 (1–3 marks).

[26] A balance of payments surplus would be good for a government to run because it means that the country is making money, which will improve living standards. A surplus is when $X > M$ and that means that the AD curve is shifting to the right. This is good because it means that when the economy is booming there is lots of growth and jobs. Firms are selling more output and so they want more workers to make their products.

The problem with this growth is that it will cause inflation. This is in the extract when it says 'a balance of payments surplus on the current account increases the level of aggregate demand into the economy' (Extract C). Inflation is bad because it erodes the value of money. Inflation is measured using the CPI, whereby a basket of goods and services enjoyed by the average family is measured by economists on a monthly basis. If prices are rising then workers can buy less with their wages. In this case it will be demand-pull inflation, which I have already explained in my earlier answer to Part 24 of this question.

Aggregate demand will be moving to the right because exports will be greater than imports. Both are components of AD which is measured using the formula $AD = C + I + G + (X - M)$.

Economic growth is good because it is one of the main economic objectives of government. It will also lead to higher employment and lower unemployment, which is also good because that too is an economic objective of government. The problem is that it will result in higher inflation, which is bad because control of inflation is an objective of government. This is a policy trade-off and for this reason a government needs to think carefully before pursing persistent current account surpluses.

If the government wants to bring down the rate of inflation it needs to introduce supply-side polices. Extract C says that if the economy is 'close to full capacity, demand-pull inflation results'. Supply-side policies will help solve this problem because they will shift $LRAS$ to the right and bring down inflation.

A government should therefore try to run current account surpluses to create growth and jobs but introduce supply-side polices to deal with the problem of inflation.

ⓔ **12/25 marks awarded.** This answer displays some knowledge of economic theory but fails to address sufficiently the set question. It is therefore placed as a low Level 3. The student does not explore the problems caused by persistent surpluses resulting in wider trade imbalances. A reasonable understanding of how export sales can stimulate employment is shown and how this can result in inflationary pressures. Points are made but not developed in chains of reasoning. Supply-side policies are mentioned but no details are given.

ⓔ **Total score: 25/50 marks = Grade C**

Question 6 How low can interest rates go? (A-level)

Note: Because this is a Context 2 data-response question, which would be preceded in an exam by a Context 1 question, the extracts are lettered D and E and the sub-parts of the question are labelled [05], [06], [07] and [08].

Context 2

Total for this Context: 40 marks

Study Extracts D and E, and then answer all parts of Context 2 which follow.

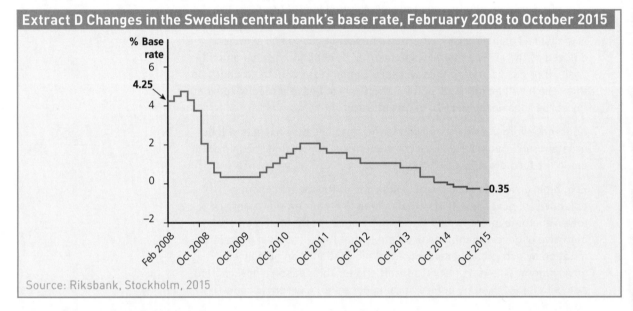

Extract D Changes in the Swedish central bank's base rate, February 2008 to October 2015

Source: Riksbank, Stockholm, 2015

Extract E Interest rate policy

For several decades in the UK, monetary policy has been used to manage the level of aggregate demand. To achieve this end, until 2009 monetary policy relied almost exclusively on the Bank of England raising or lowering Bank Rate (the Bank's 5 base rate).

To reduce aggregate demand in the 'boom' phase of the economic cycle, Bank Rate would be raised, in the hope that other interest rates would then 10 also increase, thereby reducing consumption spending and spending on imports.

Conversely, in the recessionary phase of the economic cycle, Bank Rate would be cut so as to stimulate consumption and investment spending 15 by firms. This is what happened in 2009 when Bank Rate was cut to an all-time low of 0.5%, the lowest it has been since the Bank of England was

created in 1694. Bank Rate has remained at 0.5% since then, though by 2015 Mark Carney, the Bank 20 of England's governor, had hinted that Bank Rate might soon be raised. So far, in January 2016, this has not happened.

However, using very low, and indeed negative, interest rates to stimulate aggregate demand 25 may not be very effective. In a quotation often attributed to the great economist Maynard Keynes, cutting interest rates towards zero in an attempt to stimulate economic recovery is a bit like 'pushing on a piece of string'. This is because 30 interest rate changes result in asymmetrical outcomes. Keynes argued that it is easier to eliminate excess aggregate demand by increasing interest rates than it is to end a recession by cutting interest rates. 35

Other factors can also contribute to the ineffectiveness of interest rate policy as a method of boosting aggregate demand. One of these is the problem of 'zero bound'. Once Bank Rate has been cut to zero or close to zero, it has generally been thought further cuts would be impossible to make. When a 'zero bound' base rate had been reached, central bankers believed they had run out of room to support their economies. Cut any lower, and savers face negative returns. This would encourage people to take their savings out of banks and hoard their savings in cash. Negative interest rates could slow, rather than boost, the economy.

However, central bankers in Scandinavian countries have recently thought differently.

By reducing their base rates below zero, the rates offered on bank deposits have followed. Yet rather than stuffing cash under mattresses, households have left their money in their banks or spent it. And because there is still plenty of spare capacity in their economies, inflation has not raised its ugly head.

Indeed, the Swedish Riksbank reduced its base rate below zero to try to stop deflation taking hold. It hoped that negative interest rates would stimulate spending in the Swedish economy by causing the Krona's exchange rate to fall. This in turn would increase the international competitiveness of Swedish industries and cause demand for Sweden's exports to rise.

Source: News reports, 2016

[05] Using the data in Extract D, calculate to one decimal place the percentage change in the Swedish Riksbank's base rate between February 2008 and October 2015. [2 marks]

ⓔ Note that the Swedish central bank's base rate fell over the whole of the data period. This will affect your calculation.

[06] Explain how the changes shown in Extract D in the Swedish central bank's base rate may have affected the level of aggregate demand in Sweden over the period covered by the data. [4 marks]

ⓔ Only 4 out of 40 marks can be awarded for your answer to this question. You must resist the temptation to write a long essay-style answer. Spend a maximum of 8 minutes on your answer, and preferably a little less.

[07] Lines 13–16 of Extract E state: 'in the recessionary phase of the economic cycle, Bank Rate would be cut so as to stimulate consumption and particularly investment spending by firms'.

With the aid of an *AD/AS* diagram, explain how a cut in Bank Rate can affect the level of equilibrium national income in an economy. [9 marks]

ⓔ Make sure you develop your answer beyond a statement that a cut in Bank Rate increases aggregate demand. You must include a 'logical chain of reasoning' as to why this is so. Also, you must take account of the shape of the *SRAS* curve.

[08] Lines 24–26 of Extract E state: 'using very low, and indeed negative, interest rates to stimulate aggregate demand may not be very effective'.

Using the data in the extracts and your economic knowledge, evaluate the case for a central bank to reduce its base rate below zero. [25 marks]

ⓔ Because this is a new and difficult topic, not well covered in textbooks, a number of 'prompts' for you to draw on have been included in Extract E.

> **Student A**
>
> **[05]** In February 2008 the Swedish base rate was 4.25%. By October 2015, it had fallen to the negative value of −0.35%, a fall of 4.6% in total. The change over the whole period was minus 4.6% divided by 4.25% and then multiplied by 100. This is a change of minus 108.23529%, which rounded to one decimal place is minus 108.2%.

ⓔ **2/2 marks awarded.** The answer is correct and all the working of the calculation is shown.

> **[06]** Between February 2008 and October 2015 the Swedish central bank increased the base rate of interest twice and cut it twice. Interest rates were cut quickly between the summer of 2008, when they were at 4.75%, and January 2009 when they were 0.25%. The bank nudged rates up slowly at the beginning of 2010 to 2% by the end of the year but then started cutting them in the autumn of 2011. In October 2014 interest rates turned negative.
>
> When the Riksbank cut interest rates it was trying to stimulate aggregate demand. The bank rate determines the cost of borrowing in an economy, therefore by cutting rates the bank was trying to encourage borrowing and spending and discourage saving. In contrast, when the bank raised rates it was trying to dampen spending in the economy and reduce aggregate demand. The two main components of aggregate demand that interest rates affect are consumption and investment.

ⓔ **4/4 marks awarded.** The last part of the answer earns all the marks. The earlier part is a rather long-winded statement of the ups and downs of the Swedish Bank Rate over the whole data period. It is the overall fall in Bank Rate from over 4% to the negative value of −0.35% that is important.

> **[07]** By cutting its Bank Rate the central bank is attempting to stimulate spending so that it boosts aggregate demand in the short run and creates incentives for long-term investment by firms to enhance the capacity of the economy in the long run.
>
> A cut in Bank Rate will make it cheaper for financial institutions to borrow from the central bank. High street banks should pass these savings on to their customers, households and firms, and offer them lower interest rates on loans and savings accounts. By cutting the Bank Rate the central bank's policy is designed to create incentives to increase spending and boost the level of aggregate demand.
>
> In the short run, households should increase consumption spending and firms will increase investment spending to take advantage of the low interest rates. This should increase real national income, shown in the diagram from y_1 to y_2.

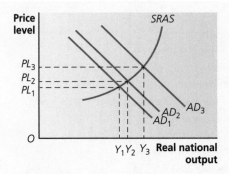

There will also be a multiplier effect which further stimulates the growth of real output (and also of the price level). The initial increase in consumption and investment brought about by the cut in Bank Rate shifts the AD curve from AD_1 to AD_2. Real national output initially increases from y_1 to y_2. However, the multiplier effect results in a further increase in aggregate demand to AD_3, with real national output increasing to y_3.

The increase in investment brought about by the expansionary monetary policy will, in the short run, increase demand in the economy. It is, however, also the engine of long-term growth. If firms take advantage of low interest rates and borrow to improve their capital infrastructure, they will become more productive. This will enhance the capacity of the economy and will create long-term growth. In the long run this will shift the $LRAS$ curve (not shown on the diagram) to the right.

e **9/9 marks awarded.** An excellent answer, which develops at least three chains of reasoning (initial increase in aggregate demand, multiplier effect and the possible effect on long-run aggregate supply).

[08] The Bank of England has set monetary policy since 1997 with the long-term aim of hitting an inflation target. The main tool in its armoury has been the UK Bank Rate, which it has used to try to manage the level of aggregate demand in the economy. The Bank Rate is the interest rate that the Bank of England charges to commercial banks, which effectively sets the cost of borrowing in the economy. In 2005 when the UK economy was seen to be overheating the Bank Rate was increased to cool the economy down by increasing the cost of borrowing. During the so-called Great Recession of 2008 and 2009, Bank Rate was cut to 0.5% in order to stimulate aggregate demand. The purpose of this policy was to 'stimulate consumption and investment spending by firms' (Extract E). This helped households with large debts, notably mortgages on their homes, to keep up with their repayments and pay down unsecured debts. However, the Bank of England did not cut interest rates to 0% in order to stimulate aggregate demand because this would not have been an effective policy. As Extract E states, 'cutting interest rates towards zero ... is a bit like "pushing on a piece of string"'. This is because cutting interest rates from 0.5% to 0% makes very little difference to the cost of borrowing, hence once the Bank Rate is close to the zero bound of 0%, a central bank has 'run out of room to support' its economy (Extract E).

In fact cutting the Bank Rate to zero might actually make things worse by slowing consumption spending and hindering economic growth. This is because zero interest rates might 'encourage people to take their savings out of banks and hoard their savings in cash' (Extract E). This is most likely to happen in a deep recession if there is uncertainty about the health of banks and fears that they may collapse. Even if savers do not withdraw their money from the banking system, zero interest rates will mean that households that depend on interest from their savings for an income will suffer a cash flow problem. Pensioner groups will be particularly hit hard by this situation and they will cut back on consumption spending as a result. Pensioner households are an increasingly significant section of the British population so if Bank Rate is set at 0% it will not only hurt these households financially but it will slow consumer spending.

The experience of the Swedish Riksbank, however, suggests that a 0% Bank Rate or negative interest rates may actually help to stimulate economic growth. According to the chart in Extract D, the Riksbank cut the Bank Rate to 0% in September 2014 and by October 2015 had reduced it to −0.35%. According to Extract E this has not led to a hoarding by households but rather an increase in consumption spending. This has stimulated aggregate demand but without the 'ugly head' of inflation appearing due to the depressed nature of the economy.

The extent to which households will decide to spend their savings when interest rates are negative may well depend on the country. Sweden is a small affluent economy and it is probable that many Swedish households could afford to spend some of their savings. The UK is a much larger country with a higher level of home ownership and a large pensioner population. Negative interest rates could encourage more buyers into the already heated housing market while forcing pensioners to spend their retirement capital. This could boost aggregate demand in the short run but create long-term problems. The housing market might overheat then crash, leading to the spectre of negative equity. If pensioners deplete their savings they will have no choice but to turn to the state for welfare support.

However, if the Bank Rate were to be cut to zero it could lead to a fall in the exchange rate and help British firms sell their products in international markets. This policy was pursued in Sweden to fight deflation and help stimulate an export-led recovery (Extract E). It may help the British economy but it is unlikely that if the Bank of England cuts interest rates from 0.5% to 0% it will have a significant effect on the exchange rate because the change in interest rate is insignificant.

Ultimately, cutting the base rate can stimulate aggregate demand but once interest rates get close to zero the effectiveness of the policy is limited. In order to stimulate a struggling economy the central bank needs to use the other tool available, the money supply, and try to inject liquidity into the financial system. The central bank also needs to work with the government, which should be running a loose fiscal policy in a recession to increase levels of disposable income and encourage spending.

(e) **22/25 marks awarded.** Once again this is an excellent answer that reaches the highest Level 5. One of its best features is continuous evaluation throughout the course of the writing. However, because the answer lacks a formal 'rounding up' conclusion' it is placed at the lower end of Level 5.

(e) **Total score: 37/40 marks = Grade A***

Student B

[05] 108.2

(e) **0/2 marks awarded.** While the number is correct, the % sign and the minus sign are missing, so both of the available marks are lost.

[06] The Bank Rate is the interest rate that the central bank lends at to commercial institutions, which in turn lend to households and firms. When the Riksbank cut the Bank Rate from 5% in August 2008 to 0.25% in January 2009, it was trying to stimulate aggregate demand. By making the cost of borrowing cheaper it was trying to increase consumption spending. It hoped that households would save less and borrow more money and this would increase aggregate demand.

When the Riksbank increased interest rates in 2010 it wanted to do the opposite. By increasing interest rates it wanted to make saving attractive and borrowing expensive. It did this to take spending out of the economy and decrease the level of aggregate demand.

(e) **3/4 marks awarded.** In general, this is an accurate and succinct answer providing a good overview without getting bogged down in detail. However, a mark is lost because the answer does not address the words in the question 'over the period covered by the data'. The fall in the Swedish Bank Rate from October 2011 onwards and the fact that it became negative in 2014 are not discussed.

[07] If the central bank wants to cut the base rate it will make borrowing money cheaper. This will mean that households and businesses will want to save less and borrow more. Spending will increase and C and I will go up. This will mean that AD shifts to the right. This is drawn in the diagram below. This will increase the level of equilibrium from y_1 to y_2.

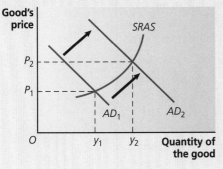

This is demand-side growth because *AD* has shifted to the right. As the diagram shows, it will increase the quantity of goods produced in the economy, but it will also increase demand-pull inflation, which is good and bad for the economy. Growth is good but inflation is bad. This is known as an economic trade-off. Inflation will occur because firms' costs of production rise to increase production. That is why a good's price increases from P_1 to P_2. If the government wants to reduce the price level it can only do this by introducing supply-side policies such as education and training. If it introduces supply-side polices it will bring down inflation but this will be in the long run. Cutting the Bank Rate will affect the level of aggregate demand in the short run and will lead to a higher equilibrium level of national income.

ⓔ **6/9 marks awarded.** This answer develops a valid chain of reasoning (effect of a Bank Rate cut on aggregate demand), but then drifts away from the question. The answer lacks discussion of the impact of the shape of the *SRAS* curve on equilibrium national income. The labelling of the diagram axes is also wrong.

[08] Bank Rate is used in the setting of interest rates in an economy. In the UK the Bank of England sets Bank Rate or the base rate, whereas in the eurozone it is the ECB, the Federal Reserve in the USA and in Japan the Bank of Japan. Central banks use interest rates to manage the level of aggregate demand in order to hit an inflation rate target, currently 2% in the UK.

If a central bank needs to increase the level of demand in the economy, to raise aggregate demand, it will cut interest rates. By cutting interest rates it will create an incentive for people to spend money. If people spend more money, consumption increases. Consumption is a component of aggregate demand so if consumption goes up then *AD* will shift to the right. In the extract it says 'in the recessionary phase of the economic cycle, Bank Rate would be cut so as to stimulate consumption and investment by firms'. This is why the Bank of England has cut interest rates to 0.5%. Therefore it makes sense for it to cut interest rates further to shift *AD* to the right if they need to.

This worked in Scandinavian countries because when interest rates were cut below 0%, households spent. People are rational and it makes no sense to keep money in a bank account if you do not get interest on it. Therefore, a central bank should cut interest rates to minus to get people to spend their money. This will create economic growth.

According to the extract the economist Maynard Keynes said that cutting interest rates would not work because it was like 'pushing on a piece of string'. This does not make sense because in countries like Sweden and Switzerland where interest rates have turned negative their economies have grown. Negative interest rates will encourage households to spend money and not to save.

> Furthermore, if interest rates are negative this will lower the exchange rate. This will create 'international competitiveness' and help the country have an export-led recovery. This will be good for economic growth because *AD* will shift to the right and GDP will increase. It will also create more jobs, which is a significant macroeconomic objective.
>
> To conclude, the central bank should cut interest rates to stimulate economic growth and it should not worry about them turning negative. Countries that have done this have grown and it has worked for them so it is a good policy.

ⓔ **13/25 marks awarded.** This answer reaches mid-Level 3. It needs greater theoretical explanation of the chains of reasoning briefly mentioned, but not really developed. Evaluation is rather thin, especially in the two-sentence conclusion, which relies on assertion rather than on final justification of points made earlier in the answer.

ⓔ **Total score: 22/40 marks = Grade C**

Knowledge check answers

1 Economic growth is measured by the percentage rate of growth of real GDP over a 12-month period.

2 Inflation is defined as the percentage increase in the average price level over a particular period, usually a year. By contrast, deflation is defined as the percentage decrease in the average price level over a particular period, usually a year. Disinflation is defined as the slowing down over a particular period of a positive rate of inflation.

3 Net domestic product (NDP) equals the gross domestic product (GDP) minus depreciation on a country's capital goods. Domestic product is the part of national income produced within the economy.

4 An advantage of expressing economic data in index numbers is that real values, undistorted by the effect of changes in the price level, can be accurately measured.

5 Figure 3 shows two flows of income circulating round the economy. The inner dashed lines in the diagram show the real flows of goods and services and the supply of factor services being exchanged in the economy. The outer solid lines show how nominal income or money flows paid by firms to members of households circulates back to the firms when spent on the goods and services the firms have sold to them. For the nominal flow of income and spending to be complete, withdrawals of spending out of the circular flow must be matched by injections of spending into the flow.

6 Aggregate demand is defined as total *planned* spending on real output by all the economic agents in the economy. By contrast, national expenditure measures *actual* or *realised* expenditure on national output, for example in a past year.

7 Macroeconomic equilibrium occurs at the level of real output at which total planned spending on real output equals the real output which firms wish to supply. *Aggregate* demand equals *aggregate* supply (*AD* = *AS*). By contrast, microeconomic equilibrium occurs at the *disaggregated* level in a single market within the economy, when planned demand for a good or service equals planned supply.

8 On the demand side of the economy, a cut in the rate of income tax shifts the *AD* curve to the right. On the supply side of the economy, by increasing incentives for people to work harder and to be more entrepreneurial, the *LRAS* curve shifts rightward.

9 Consumption is total planned spending by members of households on consumer goods and services. Saving is disposable income which is not consumed. Investment is total planned spending by firms and other producers within the economy on capital goods.

10 An increase in the rate of interest causes households to save rather than to consume. Firms often borrow funds to finance investment in new capital goods. An increase in the rate of interest raises the cost of borrowing and reduces investment. When the rate of interest falls, the opposite happens.

11 The investment multiplier and the accelerator both relate to the relationship between investment and national income, but they work in opposite directions. With the multiplier, a change in investment leads to a change in national income. With the accelerator, a change in national income affects the level of investment.

12 The economic cycle is often called the business cycle, and an old-fashioned name can also be used: the trade cycle.

13 Frictional unemployment, also known as transitional unemployment, occurs in the time delay when workers are switching between jobs. Structural unemployment is long-term unemployment occurring when some industries are declining, even though other industries may be growing.

14 A budget deficit run by the government is an injection of spending into the circular flow of income. It increases aggregate demand. By contrast, a balance of payments deficit on current account is a leakage or withdrawal of spending from the circular flow. It decreases aggregate demand.

15 A policy conflict occurs when it is impossible to achieve two or more policy objectives at the same time. A policy trade-off is an attempt to resolve the conflict by achieving satisfactory, though not perfect, performance with regard to the conflicting objectives.

16 Each month households with large mortgages pay interest on their mortgages to the bank or building society from which they have borrowed. An increase in mortgage interest rates raises the cost of borrowing, leaving mortgagees with less disposable income to spend on consumption.

17 Both multipliers measure the relationship between a change in the particular component of aggregate demand (government spending or investment) and the resulting change in nominal national income. If any of the other components of aggregate demand change (consumption or exports), there will be a multiplier effect. These multipliers are called the consumption multiplier and the export multiplier. There are also tax and import multipliers, but since these result from leakages of aggregate demand from the circular flow of income, they are negative multipliers.

18 For a supply-side economist, the term 'crowding in' refers to the need to cut the size of the public sector in order to free resources for the private sector to

use. 'Crowding in' is the opposite of 'crowding out', which occurs (according to supply-side economists) when growth of the public sector stifles or displaces private sector activity.

19 In a progressive tax system, the proportion of a person's income paid in tax increases as income rises, while in a regressive tax system, the proportion paid in tax falls as income increases.

20 Supply-side economists support income tax cuts not to increase aggregate demand, but to create supply-side incentives for people to work harder, to be entrepreneurial, and to save and invest.

21 One of the main ways of increasing competitiveness and efficiency is to increase labour productivity (output per worker) and capital productivity (output per unit of capital). Indeed, without such productivity increases, it is largely impossible to increase cost competitiveness within the economy.

Index

Note: Page numbers in **bold** font indicate key terms.

Index